DECORATIVE PAINTING

Gretchen Cagle's
DECORATIVE PAINTING
KEEPSAKES

NORTH LIGHT BOOKS
CINCINNATI, OHIO

Biography

Gretchen Cagle, after twenty-four years of tole and decorative painting, continues to be one of the industry's leading designers, as well as a teacher, publisher and author. The fourteen books and seven videos in her highly acclaimed *Heart to Heart* series have inspired thousands of decorative artists. Countless others have admired and painted Gretchen's designs, which have appeared in *Good Housekeeping, Decorative Artist's Workbook, The Decorative Painter, Craftworks for the Home, Family Circle/Great Ideas Christmas Helps, Redbook* and *Better Homes and Gardens Crafts Showcase.*

Gretchen has received recognition as a Certified Decorative Artist through the National Society of Tole and Decorative Painters, an organization of thirty thousand members. She was the 1985-1986 president and received the coveted Dedicated Service Award in 1994.

Gretchen maintains an active seminar schedule. In addition to teaching nationally and internationally, she teaches weekly classes in Tulsa, Oklahoma.

Gretchen is actively involved in her publishing company, a leading producer of instructional material within the decorative painting industry. Over twenty-five of the most recognized decorative artists in the United States have chosen her company to publish and distribute their books.

Gretchen Cagle's Decorative Painting Keepsakes. Copyright © 1997 by Gretchen Cagle. Manufactured in China. All rights reserved. No part of this book may be reproduced in any form or by any electronic or mechanical means including information storage and retrieval systems without permission in writing from the publisher, except by a reviewer, who may quote brief passages in a review. Published by North Light Books, an imprint of F&W Publications, Inc., 1507 Dana Avenue, Cincinnati, Ohio 45207. (800) 289-0963. First edition.

Other fine North Light Books are available from your local bookstore, art supply store or direct from the publisher.

01   00   99   98   97   5   4   3   2   1

Library of Congress Cataloging-in-Publication Data

Cagle, Gretchen.
    Gretchen Cagle's decorative painting keepsakes / Gretchen Cagle.—1st ed.
        p.   cm.
    Includes index.
    ISBN 0-89134-835-2 (alk. paper)
    1. Painting. 2 Painted woodwork. 3. Decoration and ornament—Plant forms. I. Title.
TT385.C344   1997
745.7'23—dc21   97-1899
                                                                                    CIP

Edited by Jennifer Long
Production Edited by Michelle Kramer
Interior and cover designed by Brian Roeth

The materials in this compilation appeared in the following pamphlets previously published by Gretchen Cagle Publications, Inc. *Heart to Heart . . . Made Easy; Heart to Heart . . . Country Style; Heart to Heart . . . Decorated With Elegance; Heart to Heart . . . A Country Collection; Heart to Heart . . . The Essence of Summer; Heart to Heart . . . Painted Treasures; Heart to Heart . . . With Simple Pleasures; Heart to Heart . . . Floral Accents.*

North Light Books are available for sales promotions, premiums and fund-raising use. Special editions or book excerpts can also be created to specification. For details contact: Special Sales Manager, F&W Publications, 1507 Dana Avenue, Cincinnati, Ohio 45207.

Contents

PART ONE

Fruit—Instant Heirlooms

Before You Begin

BRUSHES

Winsor & Newton Series 710—Use these red sable, short-bristle flats (sometimes called *brights*) in sizes 2 through 12 for color application and blending. All brushes should have sharp, clean, chisel edges that hold together even after applying and blending paint. Poor chisel edges will yield fuzzy edges on design elements and will be difficult to blend with.

Winsor & Newton Series 3A—Use these small, red sable rounds in sizes 0 to 1 to create all line work and pollen dots, and for small, detailed areas.

You can substitute any excellent-quality red sable flats, liners or round brushes for the brushes mentioned above. Synthetics may also be used; however, they quickly become saturated with paint and painting mediums due to their lack of resiliency. If you decide to use synthetic brushes, have several of each size available. When a brush no longer snaps back to its original flat, chisel-edge shape, clean it in odorless brush cleaner and lay it aside for several days before using it again.

PAINTS

Most of the designs in this book are painted with Winsor & Newton Alkyd or Oil Colors. Oils and alkyds are totally compatible; therefore, the same mediums and varnishes may be used with both, and they may be used together on the same palette and intermixed with each other. Since alkyd colors dry more quickly than oil colors, the higher the pro-portion of alkyd color in a mixture, the more quickly the colors will dry. If you're using an all-alkyd palette, the colors will be workable for approximately forty-five minutes, at which point they may become too tacky for you to do any additional blending. If you use an all-alkyd palette, work and complete small areas of the design at a time. Alkyd colors will be completely dry in eighteen hours, and will often be dry in ten to twelve hours, depending on climatic conditions and air movement over the painting surface.

MISCELLANEOUS SUPPLIES

- Designs From the Heart wood sealer
- No. 400 grit silicon carbide sandpaper
- Facial tissue
- Assorted bottled acrylic basecoat colors
- Krylon Matte Finish Spray, no. 1311
- Tracing paper
- Gray graphite paper
- White graphite paper
- Stylus
- Felt-tip marker
- Technical pen and ink
- Masking tape
- Clear tape
- Winsor & Newton Blending & Glazing Medium
- Odorless brush cleaner
- Woven paper towels
- Disposable palette paper
- Cotton swabs
- Natural sea wool sponge
- Americana Crackle Medium
- Gold and copper leaf kits
- White Lightning
- 1-inch checkerboard stencil

BACKGROUND PREPARATION

1. Seal all wood surfaces with Designs From the Heart wood sealer or any other quality brush-on wood sealer.

PAINT PALETTE

Refer to the following key for abbreviations:

Winsor & Newton Alkyd or Oil Colors

AC	Alizarin Crimson
BLK	Ivory Black
BS	Burnt Sienna
BU	Burnt Umber
CL	Cadmium Lemon
CO	Cadmium Orange
CoB	Cobalt Blue
CoVH	Cobalt Violet Hue
CRD	Cadmium Red Deep
CRL	Cadmium Red Light
CRM	Cadmium Red Medium
CYD	Cadmium Yellow Deep
CYL	Cadmium Yellow Light
CYM	Cadmium Yellow Medium
DP	Dioxazine Purple
FT	Flesh Tint
FU	French Ultramarine
IR	Indian Red
LRO	Light Red Oxide or Light Red
NYH	Naples Yellow Hue
OG	Olive Green
PB	Prussian Blue

PtB	Phthalo Blue
RS	Raw Sienna
SG	Sap Green
TW	Titanium White
WO	Winsor Orange (available in oil only)
YO	Yellow Ochre

Rembrandt Oil Colors

BM	Brown Madder Alizarin
BtC	Burnt Carmine
GU	Greenish Umber
NYH	Naples Yellow Hue
NYD	Naples Yellow Deep Extra
NYL	Naples Yellow Light Extra
TOR	Transparent Oxide Red

Grumbacher Oil Colors

GL	Geranium Lake
TYG	Thalo Yellow Green

2. Sand wood surfaces when the sealer is dry.
3. Paint the item with acrylic, or stain it, using the background color of your choice.
4. Spray with Krylon Matte Finish, no. 1311, before applying your pattern.

TRANSFERRING THE PATTERN

1. Precisely trace the main design elements onto tracing paper with a felt-tip pen. Do not trace shading, tendrils, vein lines or stems on leaves.
2. Correctly position the tracing on your painting surface.
3. Secure the tracing in place with masking tape.
4. Slide a graphite sheet under the tracing.
5. With a stylus, trace the pattern onto the surface using light pressure.

TERMINOLOGY

Accent—Usually a midvalue color used to add interest and to help harmonize the overall composition.

Base—Filling in the entire area with a solid application of a single color.

Blocking in—Laying in the initial statement by broadly indicating tone, color and line.

Dark Area—Usually refers to color applied in shadows. With flowers, it is generally positioned beneath the petals. With fruit or other round objects, it normally takes the shape of a crescent and is positioned opposite the light source.

Double-Loading Your Brush—One corner or side of the brush is loaded with one color, and another color is loaded onto the other side. Before applying it to the surface, the colors should be blended on a clean area of the palette so that they are evenly distributed through either side of the brush, meeting in the middle to form a third color.

Glazing—Oil-based medium applied over a dry area to facilitate application of additional color.

Highlight—An area of brightest or most intense value on a design element. Color is built in layers, with the area covered by each application becoming smaller and lighter.

1. Load your brush with the desired color.
2. Release paint in the highlight area.
3. Dry-wipe the brush to remove excess paint. Softly blend the color, beginning around the perimeter of the highlight and then gradually moving into the center of the highlight area.
4. Repeat, using the next lightest value.

Light Area—The lightest color used to complete the block-in of an object. It is not as light, bright or as intense as the highlight, which is normally positioned over the light area.

Midvalue—Color betweeen the dark and light areas of a design element. If several midvalues are listed, apply the darkest color next to the dark area and blend. Then apply and blend each successive color next to the previously applied color.

Overcolor—Refers to the stroking of a color over an undercolor, usually to create daisy petals.

Reflected Light—Where the crescent opposite the light source on a round object does not touch the outside edge, usually painted a midvalue, often with a BLK + TW or FU + TW tint.

Resting Area—The shadow areas used to anchor a design element to the surface it rests on, giving the illusion of a tabletop or other support. These areas are normally created using horizontal strokes of color under each element.

Scumbling—Applying a scant amount of color to a dry surface to which no glazing medium has been applied. Color is applied with an old, worn brush that is then dry-wiped and used to blend or soften the color into the surrounding colors.

Shade—Color used to deepen the shadow within a dark area of the design element. On a round, top object, it is applied diagonally opposite the light source. On overlapping objects, it is used to deepen the triangular areas that form in the overlap of the elements.

1. Load a small amount of color into your brush.
2. Place the shade value in the appropriate positions within the dark area.
3. Wipe your brush.
4. Softly blend only the outside edge.

Tint—A pure color mixed with white, such as TW + FU, that is used in the reflected-light area of a round object. When a tint is not mixed with white, it means the same as *accent*.

Undercolor—The first application of a color or a combination of colors applied to an object. It normally forms soft, shadowing areas of color on the object. For instance, undercolor may be applied under daisy petals before you actually stroke on the petals. When petals are stroked over it, the undercolor bleeds through slightly.

Wipe Your Brush—Fold a very soft paper towel into several layers. Position the brush between the layers and gently press, and then pull the bristles through the towel to remove any excess paint. Wiping the brush is normally done after applying color but before blending, or when changing colors.

COLOR NOTES

When colors within an area are *listed one below the other*, use the following dry-wipe technique:

1. Apply the first color or combination listed.
2. Dry-wipe the brush. (Never clean your brush with odorless brush cleaner when changing colors.)
3. If you're making a dramatic change in value, neutralize the dry-wiped brush with YO or TW.
4. Dry-wipe your brush several more times.
5. Apply the remaining color or combination of colors in the appropriate areas and blend before continuing to the next color.

Within a highlighted or shaded area, apply the first color or combination of colors and blend. Each subsequent application of color is positioned on top of the previously applied color, is smaller in size, and is blended prior to positioning the color or combination of colors.

When applying tints in midvalue areas, apply colors adjacent to each other rather than on top of one another, unless otherwise directed.

A plus (+) indicates that colors should be brush-mixed together on the palette.

1. From the puddle of colors, pull out a small amount of the first color listed.
2. Work it into the brush.
3. With the now-loaded brush, pull the second color listed out from the puddle.
4. Work it into the brush, blending the colors together on the palette.

Repeat these steps until the desired color is achieved. Do not overload the brush. It is not necessary to mix all the color for one area: Variation will add interest.

When a color or mixture of colors is followed by the words *when dry*, allow preceding applications of color to dry, and then apply these colors using a glazing or scumbling technique.

PAINTING TECHNIQUES

When using alkyd colors, it is important to use an ample amount of paint because of their faster drying time. Load the brush fully with color so that the inner and outer bristles of the brush are evenly saturated. Apply color so that the background of the surface is evenly coated and not visible through the paint; however, do not use so much paint that it forms ridges. Apply the color with short, choppy, overlapping strokes, moving the brush in all directions. Apply each color as listed, and then blend with soft-pressure strokes before applying another color. When blending colors, allow the brush to straddle the color break and, with the same brushstroke technique, soften the color only where it touches its neighboring color. Blend only

enough to merge the colors, alleviating any defined break between them. It is not necessary to blend clear across a previously applied color: Allowing a color to blend with a color that is not adjacent to it will result in overblending and loss of value.

When the paint begins to tack up, or lifts as a color is applied on top of it, it will be necessary to apply and blend new applications of paint with heavier pressure. Applying pressure will soften the uppermost dry layer of paint and allow the newly applied color to blend with the wetter colors underneath. If the color becomes too dry before completing work in a specific area, allow the color to dry to the touch and then apply any additional color using a glazing or scumbling technique.

Depending on climatic conditions, you have only a short amount of time to work within an area. Once color has been applied to an area, you have approximately forty minutes of blending time; therefore, paint and complete a single design element before continuing.

Oil colors should be applied to the surface in the same manner as alkyds, but, because of their extended drying time, use less paint. Apply small amounts of color to the surface and stretch it to cover the design element.

Regardless of the paint you choose, always apply the highlight or lighter values to a darker value firmly and with pressure, thus ensuring maximum value change within that area.

GLAZING TECHNIQUES

Through the use of glazing techniques, you can continue to work easily over a surface that has dried. You can enhance or change any previously painted area that could benefit from additional work. Glazing techniques are especially well suited for strengthening the dark shadow area and building stronger highlights and glints, as well as adding tints to the reflected-light areas of a design element.

Glazing must be done on a surface

that is completely dry to the touch. Remember that, even though the surface feels dry, the layers of paint underneath may still be fragile. Glazing techniques are done with oil-based painting mediums, which may act as a solvent to any paint that is not completely cured and bonded to the surface. If paint lifts from the surface, allow additional drying time before continuing to work.

To glaze, wet the surface with a thin coat of Winsor & Newton Blending & Glazing Medium or any other oil-based painting medium. If the medium puddles, position a single layer of facial tissue on the surface and tap it with your fingertip. Load a small amount of the desired color into the brush and apply it to the glazed surface. Dry-wipe the brush on a paper towel and, with soft-pressure strokes, blend the color into the wet medium. Remember that value changes should be gradual and without any line of demarcation between applications of colors.

To build a very strong or intense highlight over a darker area, glaze the area and apply color similar to the dried surface color, blending it into the medium. Then, while still wet, apply a slightly lighter, more intense value, blending into the previously applied color. Continue building gradually, changing the value and intensity of color until correct.

If an area appears milky or chalky, normally caused by the addition of a color containing too much white or light pigment, correct it by applying glazing medium and then rebuilding the values gradually. Begin the correction with the last color used prior to adding the color that caused the problem, then gradually build lighter colors using less of the whitish color in the mixture. It may be necessary to apply the last combination of colors several times, using less of the white color in each application.

Fruit—

Instant

Heirlooms

Summer's Favorite Fruit

Summer's Favorite Fruit

Watermelon, blueberries and peaches are perfect for summer and for beginning painters. All have textures that make them good choices for beginning blending techniques. You only need to barely touch and soften the color breaks—too much blending and you lose the texture.

BACKGROUND PREPARATION
Seal all units with Designs From the Heart wood sealer, and sand when dry.

All hearts and the melon wedge cutout are based with DecoArt Cadmium Red. When dry, spray with Krylon Matte Finish, no. 1311. These pieces are painted freehand; therefore, a pattern does not need to be traced onto the surface.

Paint the panel for the still life with Americana Cool Neutral. Paint a 1½" border using Americana Deep Teal. Mark off three rows of ½" checkerboard squares. Paint the alternate squares using Ceramcoat Nightfall Blue. Using a dull yellow acrylic, apply a narrow band of color along the inner edge of the border. Spray the panel with Krylon Matte Finish, no. 1311. Lightly trace the pattern using gray graphite paper.

Paint the frame and heart with a black acrylic and then, following directions on the container, apply Americana Crackle Medium. Use DecoArt Cadmium Red for the overcoat of color, and watch the crackles appear. Spray the frame and the heart with Krylon Matte Finish, no. 1311.

Along the outer edges of the frame and the heart, antique with a mixture of AC + BLK alkyds. Highlight along the inner edge of the frame with CRL.

PALETTE
Winsor & Newton Alkyd Colors:
Cadmium Red Light (CRL), Cadmium Red Medium (CRM), Titanium White (TW), Naples Yellow Hue (NYH), Alizarin Crimson (AC), French Ultramarine (FU), Cadmium Red Deep (CRD), Ivory Black (BLK), Cadmium Lemon (CL), Cadmium Yellow Deep (CYD)

WATERMELON
Rind
White Area . . . . .TW
Green Area . . . . .CL + FU + BLK

Red Area
Dark Area . . . . . .CRD
Midvalue . . . . . .CRM
Light Area . . . . .CRL
Shade . . . . .AC
Highlight . . . . . .NYH + CRM + TW
Tint . . . . .TW + AC
            TW + FU when dry

Seeds
Black Seeds . . . .CRL + BLK
White Seeds . . .TW + NYH

BLUEBERRIES
Base . . . . .TW + FU + BLK
Highlight . . . . . .TW
Shade . . . . . . .BLK + FU
Re-highlight . . .TW
Tint . . . . .CL + FU + TW + BLK
            CRM
            AC
Apply all tints on a dry surface.

BLUEBERRY CENTERS
Base . . . . .BLK
Highlight . . . . . .TW + FU
Glint . . . . .TW

PEACH
Base . . . . .NYH + CL + CYD
Shade . . . . . . .AC
Highlight . . . . .NYH + TW

LEAVES

    Base. . . . . .TW + CL + BLK + FU
    Highlight . . . . . .TW + FU

JUICE PUDDLE

    Stem . . . . .TW
    Shade . . . . .Green mixes
    Tint . . . . .Watermelon colors
               Blueberry colors
    Glint . . . . .TW

RESTING AREA

Various shades of green from leaves tinted with
TW + FU

All surfaces shown are available from GCP Enterprises, P.O. Box 2104,
Claremore, OK 74018-2104. (918) 342-1080.

HOLDING THE BRUSH

Pick up the brush as if it were a pencil. Pull the tip of the brush so that it rests between your thumb and forefinger. The handle should be nearly horizontal to the surface, with the bristles resting as flat as possible on the surface, rather than on the tip of the chisel. Working off the flat of the brush allows you to take fewer strokes to fill an area, and eliminates unnecessary brushstrokes and slash marks within the painting.

LOADING THE BRUSH WITH COLOR

Fill the brush with color by touching the flat of the brush into the very outer edge of the paint. Pull just a small amount of color down onto the palette, and keep adding touches of color until the brush feels as if it were gliding across the surface. Be sure that the bristles are evenly saturated with color and that there are no ridges of paint clinging to the brush. The bristles should be filled with paint about three-fourths of the way to the ferrule. Once the brush is evenly saturated, continue to extend and pull from the initial blending area down onto the palette until just a bit of resistance is felt against the palette. Using too much paint allows for overblending of colors. Because of the faster drying time of alkyds, when reloading the brush with a mixture, it will be necessary to add additional color back into the palette mixture. The more color added to the palette mixture, the longer the mixture will remain workable.

APPLYING AND BLENDING COLOR

In large areas, apply color with short, choppy brushstrokes that overlap each other. The edges of the color where another color will join it should be irregular. Dry-wipe the brush before applying the next color. When applying the next color, again use short, choppy strokes, allowing the new color to fuzz and blend over the irregular edges of the first color. If a color break is still visible, dry-wipe the brush, allow the brush to straddle the line and blend with the same short, choppy strokes. Dry-wipe the brush, continuing to add and blend each color as it is applied, allowing each color to blend only with its neighboring color. It is critical that the dark color blend only with the next color applied, usually a midvalue, and that the midvalue blend only with the light area. Allowing darks to cross over midvalues and blend with light areas will cause severe overblending and loss of value, color and dimension within the object.

Step 2—Strengthen dark areas of the melon with AC, being sure to allow some of the original dark area to be visible. On the blueberries, create strong shadows at the bottom and along the right side of each berry. Barely blend, leaving texture. Using a small, flat brush, splotch in the berry center with an irregular star shape. Highlight the leaves and add shading to the peach.

Step 1—Loosely apply the dark area mix into the broken area of the melon, to the right side of the cut edge and randomly along the lower front edge of the melon. Touch the dark areas with midvalue and barely blend color breaks. Fill in with light color and barely blend with midvalue. After basing the berries, lighten the top and left side with TW. Base in the peach and the leaves.

Step 3—Complete the melon with highlights along the bottom of the broken area, and splotch along the left side and top of the melon. Using a small, flat brush, apply seeds, keeping them irregular in shape and size so that they appear embedded in the melon. When dry, fuzz soft blue tints on right outside edge of the melon.

On the blueberries, add a soft highlight inside the center and touch a glint of white along the edge.

Strengthen intense highlights on the left side of each berry next to the centers. When dry, apply tints using a minimal amount of paint and softening them into the berry. Tints are generally applied along the darkside, outside edges to create separation and develop color harmony.

Resting areas and juice puddles are easier done when the design elements are dry. Apply color, and skim parallel to the lower edge of the surface. Use minimal color where the juice puddle is to be painted. Apply the juice puddle in an elongated C shape. Haze stronger color into the cup of the C. Add tints and glints, and pull a thin shadow of green under the lower edge of the puddle to anchor it to the resting area.

Pears to Please

Painting pears offers the opportunity to develop a variation of the basic round shape. Any object with a pinched-in neck or hourglass shape will be painted in a similar manner. These techniques apply to everything from bottles and containers to eggplants and strawberries.

BACKGROUND PREPARATION
Follow the instructions for preparing the background for the apple surface on page 29.

PALETTE
Winsor & Newton Alkyd Colors:
Cadmium Yellow Medium (CYM), Cadmium Lemon (CL), Cadmium Yellow Deep (CYD), Ivory Black (BLK), Naples Yellow Hue (NYH), Titanium White (TW), Yellow Ochre (YO), Burnt Umber (BU)

TOP PEAR
Dark Area . . . . .YO + BLK
Midvalue . . . . . .CYM + NYH
Light Area . . . . .CL + NYH + TW
Shade . . . . .BLK + YO
Highlight . . . . . .TW + CL
Glint . . . . .TW
Tint . . . . .CYM or CYD
      TW + BLK when dry
Detail Streaks . .YO + BLK when dry

BLOSSOM-END DETAIL
Base . . . . .BLK + small amount YO
Highlight . . . . . .TW

LEAVES AND STEM
Base . . . . .TW + CL + BLK
Shade . . . . .Base mix + BLK
Add some CL if color is too dull.
Highlight . . . . . .TW + CL
      TW
Tint . . . . .Pear colors

UNDERNEATH PEAR
Base . . . . .YO + CL + BLK
Shade . . . . .YO + BLK
      BLK
Highlight . . . . . .YO + CL
      NYH + CL + TW
Tint . . . . .CYD
      TW + BLK when dry
Detail Streaks . .YO + BLK when dry

TENDRILS
Use leaf colors thinned with odorless brush cleaner. The color should be an inky consistency, but not as thin as water. Apply with a liner brush. Roll the brush into the color with the bristles horizontal to the surface, and then pull to a point. Apply the paint with minimal pressure where a thin tendril is desired, and with more pressure to create a thicker line. Thicker areas of the tendril may be highlighted with the leaf highlight color.

BANNER
Base . . . . .NYH + small amount TW
Shade . . . . .NYH + BLK
Tint . . . . .YO
Highlight . . . . . .W
Lettering . . . . . .BU when dry

A pear is actually made of two round objects—a smaller sphere on top of a larger sphere. On a round object, the dark area takes the form of a crescent; therefore, on a pear, a crescent will form on each round object. At the neck, or where the pear pinches in, the crescents will overlap, forming a triangular area. Develop this area using the dark color and, when shading, create a smaller triangular area within the dark area. To create even more fullness in each round section, develop a second, less important triangle of shading on the right side of the pear in the neck area. All other rules for creating the roundness of the apple on pages 30-31 also apply to the pear.

Cabinet available from GCP Enterprises, P.O. Box 2104, Claremore, OK 74018-2104. (918) 342-1080.

Step 1—Apply dark, medium and light areas to the top pear, and base in the underneath pear. Any transparency will be less obvious as additional colors are added. To bring the top pear forward, it should be bright and intense. To make the underneath pear recede, the color should be dull.

Step 2—On the top pear, apply shading diagonally opposite the light source and in the neck area. Using the handle end of the paintbrush or a stylus, scratch out a guideline for the blossom end, and position shading in that area. On the underneath pear, shade in the triangular area formed between the leaves and the top pear. Add a touch of shading at the bottom right side.

Step 3—Begin to build highlights on each of the pears.

Step 4—Apply stronger highlights and yellow tints. Allow to dry; apply TW + BLK tint to the reflected-light area. Thin the detail streak color with brush cleaner and apply with a liner brush.

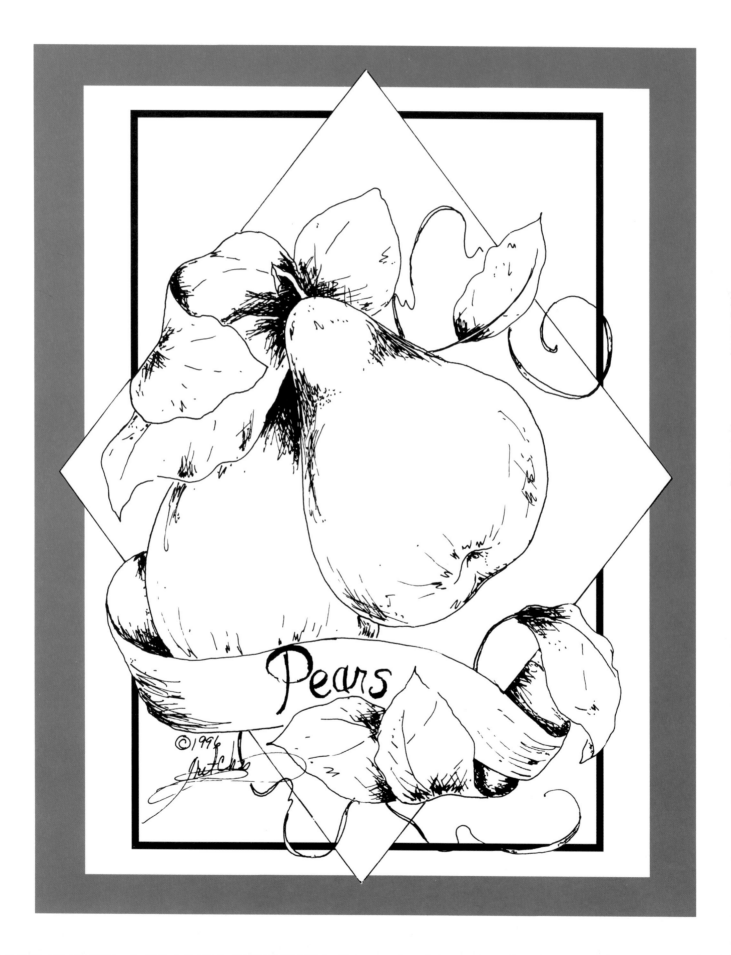

Pears

©1996

Pears and Tokay Grapes

This checkerboard is pure fun to paint. Plan to paint the pears and grapes in two sittings. At the first sitting, block in the fruit with the dark, midvalue and light areas. You might also add some highlight, as well as shading, at this time. When the fruit has dried, come back and add the strongest shading and the very brightest highlights, as well as the flecks and streaks on the pears. The reflected lights on the pears (BLK + TW), and the tints and reflected lights on the grapes (BLK + TW + PB), were all done on the dry surface. When working wet paint over a dry surface, use a minimum amount of paint and edge in with a dry brush or your finger.

BACKGROUND PREPARATION
Seal with Designs From the Heart wood sealer and sand when dry. Using a 1-inch checkerboard stencil, paint the checkboard with Ceramcoat Red Iron Oxide acrylic paint. Spray the surface with Krylon Matte Finish, no. 1311. Stain the entire surface with BU paint thinned with a small amount of odorless brush cleaner. Allow to dry, and then transfer the pattern to the surface.

PALETTE
Winsor & Newton Alkyd or Oil Colors:
Yellow Ochre (YO), Cadmium Orange (CO), Burnt Umber (BU), Cadmium Lemon (CL), Cadmium Red Light (CRL), Ivory Black (BLK), Dioxazine Purple (DP), Prussian Blue (PB), Titanium White (TW), Raw Sienna (RS)—oil only

Grumbacher Oil Colors:
Geranium Lake (GL), Thalo Yellow Green (TYG)

RIGHT PEAR
Dark Area	RS + YO
Midvalue	YO + CO
	YO
Light Area	TYG + YO
Shade	GL + BU
Highlight	TW + CL + TYG

LEFT PEAR
Dark Area	CRL + RS
Midvalue	Dark area mix + YO
Light Area	YO + CL
Shade	Dark area mix + GL + BU
Tint	CO

ALLOW PEARS TO DRY, THEN . . .
Highlight	TYG + CL + TW
	TW
Shade	GL + BU
Tint	BLK + TW
Flecks	RS + BU + GL

LIGHTEST GRAPES
Base	TYG + YO
Shade	GL
	GL + DP
Highlight	TYG
	TW

MIDVALUE GRAPES
Dark Area	GL + small amount DP + BLK
Midvalue	CRL + YO
Light Area	TYG + small amount YO
Shade	GL + DP
Highlight	TYG
	TW

DARKEST GRAPES
Base	GL + DP
Highlight	CRL
	CRL + YO

ALLOW GRAPES TO DRY, THEN . . .
Highlight just a touch brighter. Deepen shading in triangular corners.
Tint	BLK + TW + PB
	CO

LEAF #1
Dark Area	BLK + CL + small amount TW
Light Area	Dark area mix + CL + TW
Shade	Dark area mix + DP, or Dark area mix + BLK
Highlight	TW + CL

LEAF #2
Dark Area	BLK + CL + small amount RS
Midvalue	YO
Light Area	Dark area mix + CL + TW
Shade	Dark area mix + BLK + small amount GL
Highlight	TYG + small amount CL
	TW

Checkerboard available from GCP Enterprises, P.O. Box 2104, Claremore, OK 74018-2104. (918) 342-1080.

CRL + RS

TYG + YO

GL + BU

TYG + YO

YO + CL

Dk + YO

Dk + GL + BU

CO

CO

CRL + RS

TW + CL + TYG

Dk + GL + BU

TYG + Y

CO

Dk + GL + BU

CRL + RS

TYG   TW

GL+DP

GL+DP   GL

GL+DP   CRL+YO   TYG+YO

YO

GL+BU   GL+DP+BLK

YO+CO   CRL+YO

RS+YO

GL+BU

©1985

Gretchen

Follow labels for blocking in colors.
Let the painting dry, and then add detail
to the pears and grapes.

Pears and Tokay Grapes

© 1985
Gretchen

Delightfully Delicious

Apples are a staple of decorative painting because their round shape is so basic to many things we paint. Learn to paint a round object that has shape, volume and dimension, and you will be able to paint virtually anything.

BACKGROUND PREPARATION

Seal the cabinet and door with Designs From the Heart wood sealer, and sand when dry. Paint the raised panel on the door using Ceramcoat Mudstone and allow to dry. Paint the wide frame on the door with Ceramcoat Cinnamon. Paint a ½" band of Americana Light Avocado and a ½" band of Ceramcoat Cinnamon around the perimeter of the raised panel. Between the Mudstone and the Cinnamon areas, paint a thin outline with dull yellow acrylic paint. Paint the inset with Americana Soft Black. Using transparent tape as a mask will help to create clean edges for each area of color. Paint the cabinet with Cinnamon, leaving all cut edges free of paint. Paint the heart inset with Light Avocado. Spray the entire cabinet with Krylon Matte Finish, no. 1311. Antique the cabinet, including the cut edges, the wide frame and the Light Avocado band, with BU plus a small amount of Winsor & Newton Blending and Glazing Medium. Allow to dry before transferring the pattern.

PALETTE

Winsor & Newton Alkyd Colors:

Cadmium Red Medium (CRM), Cadmium Red Light (CRL), Cadmium Lemon (CL), French Ultramarine (FU), Titanium White (TW), Naples Yellow Hue (NYH), Alizarin Crimson (AC), Yellow Ochre (YO), Ivory Black (BLK), Burnt Umber (BU)

UPPER APPLE

Green Area . . . .CL + small amount FU + small
   amount YO
Dark Area . . . . .AC + YO
Midvalue . . . . . .Dark area mix + CRM + small
   amount YO
   CRM + CRL
Light Area . . . . .CRM + CRL + NYH
Shade . . . . .AC + BLK
Highlight . . . . . .NYH + TW
Tint . . . . .TW + BLK when dry
Glint . . . . .TW when dry

LOWER APPLE

Base . . . . .AC + YO
Shade . . . . .AC + BLK
Highlight . . . . . .CRM
   CRM + NYH

LEAVES AND APPLE STEM

Base . . . . .CL + BLK + TW
Add FU to some of the underneath leaves.
Shade . . . . .Base mix + BLK
Add some CL if color is too dull.
Highlight . . . . . .TW + CL
   TW
Tint . . . . .Apple colors

TENDRILS

Paint the tendrils using the leaf colors thinned with odorless brush cleaner and loaded onto a liner brush. The color should be an inky consistency, but not as thin as water. Roll the brush into the color with the bristles horizontal to the surface, and then pull to a fine point. Where a thin line is desired, apply the color with minimal pressure; use more pressure to create a thicker line. Thicker areas of the tendril may be highlighted with the highlight color from the leaf.

BANNER

Base . . . . .NYH + small amount TW
Shade . . . . .NYH + BLK
Tint . . . . .YO
Highlight . . . . . .TW
Lettering . . . . . .BU when dry

Cabinet available from GCP Enterprises, P.O. Box 2104, Claremore, OK 74018-2104. (918) 342-1080.

CREATING STREAKS ON THE APPLE

When the apple is complete but still wet, stand the brush on the chisel edge and create streaks radiating from the green area into the adjacent color. Use a dry-wiped brush without adding any color. Use minimal pressure and follow the contour of the apple. When streaking is completed, dry-wipe the brush and gently soften the streaks with the flat of the brush, again following the contour of the apple.

DEVELOPING ROUND OBJECTS

1. On a round object, the dark area takes the form of a crescent and falls opposite the light source.

2. The dark area does not touch the dark-side, outside edge of the design element. That area, known as *reflected* or *secondary light*, is always midvalue in color.

3. Midvalue color touches all dark area and may complete the perimeter of the object.

4. The light area fills the portion of the design element closest to the light source.

5. Shading makes a portion of the dark area darker in value. On a fully exposed design element, the strongest area of shading falls diagonally opposite the light source and will touch the outside edge of the element. If another design element, such as a leaf, is laid over the subject, place the darkest shading next to that overlapping object and allow the diagonally placed shaded area to be secondary. Where two objects overlap and a triangular area forms, that area will also hold the strong, dark shading. All shading colors should be cool in temperature and/or dull in intensity.

6. Highlight makes a portion of the light area lighter in value. Highlight colors should be warm in temperature and/or bright in intensity.

7. Tints are normally midvalue in color; therefore, they are placed in the midvalue areas of the element. Cool tints should be placed close to the receding area near the dark side of the design element. Warm tints should be placed in areas closer to the light source.

DEVELOPING LEAVES

Leaves usually play a supportive role in the painting; therefore, they should not be too bright in color. Using too much CL in a leaf mixture will cause the leaf to dominate the design. The use of too much TW will cause the leaf to become too dull. Use a minimal amount of paint when basing the leaf. Shading should be stronger in overlaps and at the stem end tapering toward the leaf tip. Highlight should be the strongest at the broadest part of the leaf and also taper toward the tip. Final brushstrokes should follow the growth pattern formed by the side veins as they grow away from the center vein. Paint the center vein using the base mixture, positioning it just inside the dark area. Pull side veins without reloading with color. To create a bugbite or hole: While the leaf is wet, tip a small, flat brush into odorless brush cleaner, blot on a paper towel and clean out an irregularly shaped hole. Fill the hole with the color that would normally appear in that area of the back design element or background.

Step 4—Add shading diagonally opposite the light source, and stronger shading directly under the leaf. Base the second apple, and shade in the overlaps opposite the light source.

Step 1—Since they are so easily lost, apply the green areas to the apple first. Position the dark area in a crescent form, then apply the first midvalue color, allowing it to touch in the area of reflected light. Blend.

Step 2—Apply the second mid-value color inside the crescent of the previously applied color and blend.

Step 3—Complete the apple with light area color.

Step 5—Apply highlight to the light area and begin the streaking.

Step 6—Strengthen shading and green areas, if necessary. Apply final highlights, glints and the tint to the reflected-light area.

Delightfully Delicious

Apples

©1994

Strawberries,
Sweet and Luscious

Strawberries, sweet and luscious, are the essence of springtime. Fresh, unsugared and straight from the garden they are wonderful. Add pure whipped cream and buttery yellow cake—well, that's stupendous!

BACKGROUND PREPARATION

Seal all wood surfaces with Designs From the Heart wood sealer, and sand when dry. Paint the noteboard and the strawberry plate with DecoArt Napa Red. The canvas-covered recipe file is available in black. When the painting is completed, paint around the outer edges of this design with green leaf mixtures. After preparing the background, spray all surfaces with Krylon Matte Finish, no. 1311. Transfer the patterns with white graphite paper.

PALETTE
Winsor & Newton Alkyd Colors:

Cadmium Red Medium (CRM), Titanium White (TW), Ivory Black (BLK), Cadmium Lemon (CL), French Ultramarine (FU), Alizarin Crimson (AC)

GREEN-TINTED STRAWBERRIES

Dark Area . . . . .AC
Midvalue . . . . . . .CRM
Light Area . . . . .CL + small amount FU + TW
Shade . . . . .AC + BLK
Highlight . . . . . .TW
Tint . . . . .TW + FU when dry

LIGHT RED STRAWBERRIES

Dark Area . . . . .CRM
Light Area . . . . .CRM + TW
Shade . . . . .AC
Highlight . . . . . .TW
Tint . . . . .TW + FU when dry

Continued on page 36.

strawberries, sweet and luscious

Skill Builders

Strawberries easily relate to apples in that the colors can be so similar. But they also relate to pears: Check out their shape.

While some berries may have a round shape, others may be just the reverse of a pear. They have a large top and a small bottom with a pinched-in neck; therefore, the same rules apply for building their shape. With their multiple-leafed tops, there are many smaller triangular corners for shading.

On the dark side of the berry, use the shading color in the area between the leaves; however, as you approach the lighter areas, the shading becomes lighter in value. Keep the tops as free-form and flyaway as possible. Rather than positioning seeds in the berry, which can make small berries appear overworked, apply frosting and texture with the corner of a flat brush or with a liner brush. Start in the highlight area using the highlight color, and work to the darker areas until the brush runs out of color, allowing the texture to diminish toward the dark area. In a very large berry, you may need to apply texture with the midvalue color as well.

strawberries, sweet and luscious

Continued from page 34.

DARK RED STRAWBERRIES
Dark Area . . . . .AC
Midvalue . . . . . .CRM
Light Area . . . . .CRM + TW
Shade . . . . . . .AC + BLK
Highlight . . . . . .TW
Tint . . . . .TW + FU

GREEN STRAWBERRIES
Base. . . . . .CL + small
            amounts of TW
            and FU
Shade . . . . .CL + FU
Highlight . . . . . .TW
Tint . . . . .Strawberry colors

LEAVES AND STRAWBERRY TOPS
Base. . . . . .CL + FU + BLK +
            small amount TW
Shade . . . . .CL + FU + BLK
Highlight . . . . . .TW
Tint . . . . .TW + FU
            Strawberry colors

BLOSSOMS
Base. . . . . .TW
Shade . . . . .FU + BLK
Highlight . . . . . .TW

BLOSSOM CENTERS
Base. CL
Stamens . . . . . .CL + BLK
Pollen . . . . .CL + BLK

RIBBON
Base. . . . . .CRM
Shade . . . . .AC + BLK
Highlight . . . . . .TW
Tint . . . . .TW + BLK when
            dry

Noteboard available from GCP Enterprises, P.O. Box 2104, Claremore, OK 74018-2104. (918) 342-1080.

Black canvas recipe file available from Creations in Canvas, 267 Douglass Street, Brooklyn, NY 11217. (718) 852-6969.

Strawberry plate available from Custom Wood Products, 2816 Newsome Circle, Wichita Falls, TX 76308. (817) 692-0950.

This pattern is for the lower section of the noteboard and attaches to the pattern on the next page.

© 1995

Use this pattern for the top of the noteboard. The lower section of the noteboard pattern is on the previous page.

Step 1—Base in each berry and barely blend, by tapping with the corner of a flat brush, to begin to create the texture.

Step 2—Apply shading and develop the triangular areas forming in the neck of the berry. On any berries that have a basic round shape, develop the shading in a crescent form.

Step 3—Apply highlights developing with texture. As highlight approaches the darker areas, pick up a small amount of red, gradually allowing the texture to diminish toward the dark areas. Apply tint color to the reflected light area. The ribbon is tinted with a cool color near the shaded areas: Cool tints will cause these areas to recede.

The Birdhouse Collection

BACKGROUND PREPARATION

Seal all surfaces with Designs From the Heart wood sealer, and sand when dry. Each of the houses was based with an acrylic color. I then cut lacy paper napkins and doilies to use as a stencil for the gingerbread trim. The stencils were sprayed with a spray-mount adhesive and positioned on the birdhouse. Next, I sprayed over the stenciled area with a contrasting spray paint, allowing the spray to drift over the sides and fronts of the houses.

PALETTE
Winsor & Newton Alkyd or Oil Colors:

Titanium White (TW), Cadmium Lemon (CL), Ivory Black (BLK), Naples Yellow Hue (NYH), Alizarin Crimson (AC), Dioxazine Purple (DP), French Ultramarine (FU), Cadmium Red Deep (CRD), Cadmium Red Medium (CRM), Yellow Ochre (YO)

ALL LEAVES
    Base.........TW + CL +
                 BLK
    Shade ....Base mix + BLK
    Highlight.....TW
    Tint ....Fruit colors

ALL DAISIES
    Undercolor ....BLK + small
                  amount fruit
                  colors
    Overcolor .....TW + NYH
    Shade ....Undercolor
    Highlight......TW
    Tint ....Fruit colors

DAISY CENTERS
    Base.........CL + NYH
    Shade ....AC + DP
    Highlight......TW
    Tint ....Fruit colors

BLACKBERRY BIRDHOUSE

Base the house with FolkArt Amish Blue, and spray stenciled area with flat white. Trim and accent the house with a mixture of DP + FU + TW.

Berries
    Base mix ......FU + DP +
                  BLK + AC
    Vary the mixtures so that the berries are different colors.
    Highlight......TW
    Shade ....Base color to
                  separate the
                  seeds.
    Glints ....TW

All birdhouses available from GCP Enterprises, P.O. Box 2104, Claremore, OK 74018-2104. (918) 342-1080.

CHERRY BIRDHOUSE

Base the overhang with off-white acrylic, and the remainder with Delta Dusty Plum. Spray stenciled area with Accent Country Colors Garden Rose. Antique the roof and bottom trim with AC + DP + CRD.

Darkest Cherry Below Daisy

Dark Area . . . . .AC + DP
Light Area . . . . .CRD
Shade . . . . .AC + DP +
                    BLK
Highlight. . . . . .TW + AC
                    TW
Tint . . . . .FU + TW

Remaining Cherries

Dark Area . . . . .AC + DP
Midvalue . . . . . .CRD
Light Area . . . . .Midvalue + TW
Shade . . . . .DP + small
                    amount BLK
Highlight. . . . . .TW + AC
                    TW
Tint . . . . .TW + FU

STRAWBERRY BIRDHOUSE

Base side of the house with DecoArt Flesh, and then spray the stenciled area with Accent Country Colors Roseberry. Paint the roof with Delta Wedgewood Green. Trim the eaves with Delta Rosemist.

Strawberry With Waterdrop

Dark Area . . . . .AC + NYH
Midvalue . . . . . .CRM + NYH
Light Area . . . . .TW + NYH +
                    small amount
                    CL
Shade . . . . .AC + DP +
                    small amount
                    YO
Highlight. . . . . .TW
Tint . . . . .TW + DP +
                    BLK

For all other berries, omit the CL in the light area and vary the shading. Keep the right center berry lighter, with no shading. Shade the upper left berry very dark and omit the YO.

The Birdhouse Collection

All birdhouses available from GCP
Enterprises, P.O. Box 2104, Claremore, OK
74018-2104. (918) 342-1080.

Blue Velvet Blossoms and Berries

Blue Velvet Blossoms and Berries

BACKGROUND PREPARATION

This tin sconce was spray-painted with Accent Country Colors Stoneware Blue. When using spray paints for your background, allow several days for the paint to cure before beginning the painting. If the background has not cured the mediums from the paint will act as a solvent, causing the background to lift and drag.

PALETTE

Winsor & Newton Alkyd or Oil Colors:

Prussian Blue (PB), Burnt Sienna (BS), Titanium White (TW), Yellow Ochre (YO), Cadmium Lemon (CL), Ivory Black (BLK)

Rembrandt Oil Colors:

Naples Yellow Light Extra (NYL), Brown Madder Alizarin (BM)

BLOSSOMS

Base.	NYL
Shade	PB + small amount BS
Highlight.	TW
Tint	BM
	PB + BS + TW
	YO on dark flower only.

Keep the front flower lighter and more defined. When painting the back flower, let the tints cover larger areas so that the flower will appear darker and relate more closely in value to the background.

CENTERS

Base.	YO
Shade	BM
Highlight.	CL + TW
Splotches.	BLK + TW + BM

LEAVES

Base.	CL + TW + BLK (pale gray-green)
Shade	Base mix + BLK, or Base mix + BLK + PB
Highlight.	Base mix + TW TW
Tint	BM
	BLK + TW
	PB + TW

BLUEBERRIES

Dark Area	PB + BLK + small amount TW
Light Area	Dark area mix + TW
Shade	Dark area mix + BLK + PB
Highlight.	TW
Tint	BM
	BM + TW

When applying tint to the berries, you will be more successful in achieving a rich burgundy if you let the berries dry before applying the color. Remember that BM and PB are complementary colors and will dull each other.

When completely finished with the painting, antique the left side of the heart with a deep blue-gray mixture from your palette, and flyspeck with a soft blue-gray mixture.

Daisies and Black Cherries

My father loves ice cream. As a child I remember always having a supply in the freezer. I'll never forget hot summer days and his black cherry ice cream swirled with bits of dark fruit. This surface is one that has great flexibility; you may choose to use it as a mirror frame rather than as a serving plate.

BACKGROUND PREPARATION

Seal with Designs From the Heart wood sealer. Sand when dry, and then basecoat with FolkArt Raspberry Wine. Spray lightly with Krylon Matte Finish, no. 1311. When the paint is dry, antique around the outer edge of the surface and next to the upper cherries with AC + BLK.

PALETTE

Winsor & Newton Alkyd Colors:
Cadmium Lemon (CL), Titanium White (TW), Ivory Black (BLK), Cobalt Blue (CoB), Alizarin Crimson (AC), Cadmium Red Deep (CRD), Yellow Ochre (YO)

DAISIES

Undercolor . . . .BLK + CoB + AC
Overcolor . . . . .TW + small amount YO
Shade . . . . .BLK + AC + CoB
Tint . . . . .CRD + AC
                 CoB + TW + small amount
                 BLK
Dots . . . . .BLK
                 CoB + TW
Highlight. . . . . .TW

DAISY CENTERS

Base. . . . . .YO + small amount CRD
Shade . . . . .CRD
                 CRD + CoB
Highlight. . . . . .CL + TW
Tint . . . . .CoB + TW when dry

LIGHT CHERRIES

Base. . . . . .CRD + small amount CoB
Shade . . . . .CoB + AC
Highlight. . . . . .AC + TW
Tint . . . . .CoB + TW
Glints . . . . .TW

DARK CHERRIES

Base. . . . . .CoB + CRD
Highlight. . . . . .AC + TW
Tint . . . . .CoB + TW
Glint . . . . .TW

You may need to build the highlights several times in order to achieve the necessary brightness on each of the cherries. The first application of highlight should be AC-dominant, with minimal TW. Add more TW to the second application of highlight.

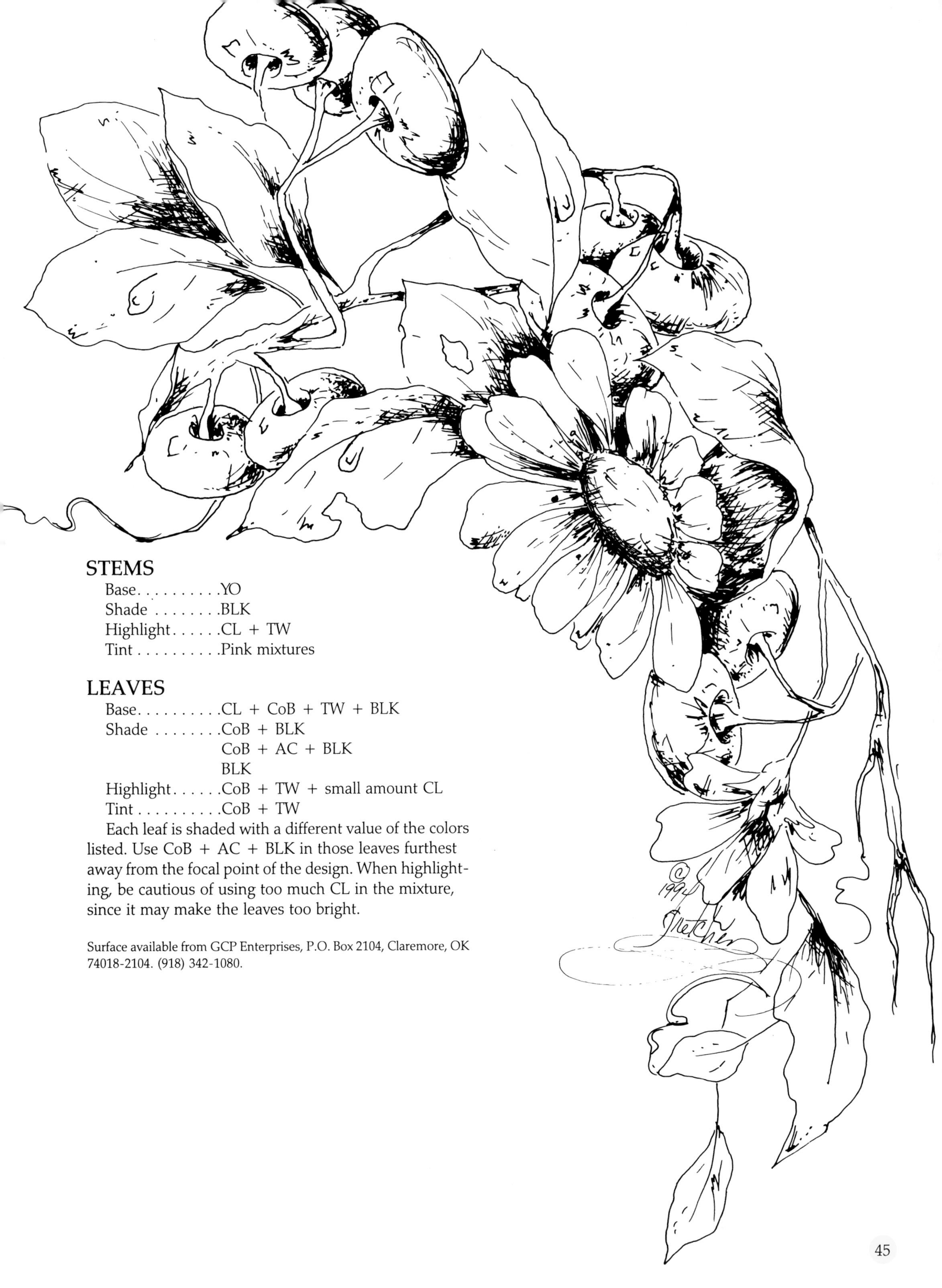

STEMS

Base . . . . YO
Shade . . . . BLK
Highlight . . . . . . CL + TW
Tint . . . . Pink mixtures

LEAVES

Base . . . . CL + CoB + TW + BLK
Shade . . . . CoB + BLK
                      CoB + AC + BLK
                      BLK
Highlight . . . . . . CoB + TW + small amount CL
Tint . . . . CoB + TW

Each leaf is shaded with a different value of the colors listed. Use CoB + AC + BLK in those leaves furthest away from the focal point of the design. When highlighting, be cautious of using too much CL in the mixture, since it may make the leaves too bright.

Surface available from GCP Enterprises, P.O. Box 2104, Claremore, OK 74018-2104. (918) 342-1080.

Daisies and Black Cherries

Plums and Daisies

If you love tole and decorative painting, you must love daisies. These country classics are as fresh as springtime and as endless as the sky in their variety and color, presenting ample opportunity for painting-skill growth. When combined with black plums against a black background, they become pure drama.

Skill Builders

Paint daisies with a flat brush, stroking each side of the petal, and then lightly blending over the strokes. Using a flat brush will create petals with each tip a different shape. Position one of the strokes further from the flower center and the other closer, and the tip will become rag-ged and irregular, creating variety within the flower. Pull the stroke from the outer edge to the center. Apply pressure at the tip of the petal and gradually let up on the pressure, pulling to a taper at the flower center.

The challenge is to create white daisies against a dark background and harmonize them with the plums and the background. All of these elements are a part of the total painting, and each must relate to the other.

The whiteness of the daisies is expressed in their highlighted areas. Strong contrast is created by the extreme dark where petals attach to the flower center or tuck under another design element. Further contrast is created with the shading and darker tint colors applied to the petal edges next to the background.

Continued on page 48.

Plums and Daisies

If necessary, strengthen the white overcolor where petals reach their highest forward arc and begin the inward curve to the flower center.

Strong tints of dull plum colors along the lower petal edges bring the daisies into harmony with the plums and add the darker background values into the flower. Keep the orange-red tints sparse.

Keep the plums very dark in value and low-key in intensity. The reflected-light color will pull them forward, away from the background. Highlights are built gradually. Begin with a color slightly brighter and redder than the basecoat. The second application of highlight should bring the plums more into the foreground and make them still lighter in value. The final highlights build to the red-orange colors and are positioned closest to the light source. Each area of highlight should be smaller than the previously applied highlight color, allowing each color to be visible. Any loss of color is a loss of value and dimension within the plum. Always reinforce any area where color is lost.

Additional harmony is created when the box is trimmed in a dull red-violet plum color. Notice that the plum colors are repeated throughout the design and the background, bringing every element into harmony.

BACKGROUND PREPARATION

Seal with Designs From the Heart wood sealer, and sand when dry. Base the entire lid with any black acrylic. Paint a ½" border along the outer edge of the top of the box and the lower portion of the box using FolkArt Black Plum. Spray with Krylon Matte Finish, no. 1311. Antique the Black Plum areas of the lid with a mixture of LRO + AC. When finished with the painting, flyspeck the box and the upper corners of the lid with various red-orange mixtures from the palette.

PALETTE

Winsor & Newton Alkyd Colors:

Cadmium Red Deep (CRD), Light Red Oxide (LRO), Cadmium Lemon (CL), Dioxazine Purple (DP), Titanium White (TW), Phthalo Blue (PtB), Ivory Black (BLK)

PLUMS

Base.........CRD + DP + a small amount PtB
Highlight......CRD
                TW + CRD + very small amount
                DP
                LRO
Shade ....BLK
Tint ....BLK + TW when dry

DAISIES

Undercolor ....BLK
Overcolor .....TW
Shade ....BLK
Tint ....DP + CRD—if necessary, add BLK
           to dull the color.
           LRO

DAISY CENTERS

Base.........LRO
Shade ....DP + CRD
Highlight......TW + CRD
Pollen ....BLK
           LRO

LEAVES

Base.........TW + CL + BLK
Shade ....Base mix + BLK
           Base mix + DP + BLK
Highlight......TW + BLK
Tint ....Plum colors

RESTING AREA

Base.........BLK
Tint ....DP + CRD
Water ....TW

Surface available from Cedar Crest, P.O. Box 387, Pleasanton, KS 66075. (913) 352-6706.

©1995 Gretchen

Step 1—Develop the plum with dull, low-key colors that barely create definition against the background. After basecoating, shade inside the crevice and add shading to form the crescent along the lower edge of the plum, being sure to leave some of the base color in the reflected-light area. Highlight with CRD along the front right lobe, just below the crevice on the front of the plum, and along the top and left side immediately against the background. Using a flat brush, apply the first stroke to a daisy petal. Before continuing to the next petal, refer to step 2 and position the second stroke on the daisy petal.

Step 2—Using a small amount of TW + CRD + a very small amount of DP, reinforce all high-light areas.

Step 3—Add soft LRO highlights on the right side of the plum and along the left edge of the plunge line. Allow the second highlight to remain visible in the center area of the plunge line. On the daisy petals, blend slightly where two strokes are obvious. Add any shading necessary to create sep-aration between the petals.

Step 4—Strengthen LRO highlights on the plums. Add the BLK + TW tint, creating a dull-gray reflected light against the outer edges of the plum. Add additional shading, overcolor high-lights and tints to the daisies.

Step 1

Step 2

Step 3

Step 4

51

Plum Country

BACKGROUND PREPARATION

Spray-paint this metal lampshade with Accent Country Colors Antique White. Allow a minimum of twenty-four hours drying time after spraying the last coat before tracing the pattern.

PALETTE

Winsor & Newton Alkyd or Oil Colors:

Titanium White (TW), Cadmium Red Light (CRL), Cadmium Red Medium (CRM), Cadmium Orange (CO), Yellow Ochre (YO), Dioxazine Purple (DP), Ivory Black (BLK), Prussian Blue (PB), Raw Sienna (RS)—oil only

Grumbacher Oil Colors:

Thalo Yellow Green (TYG), Geranium Lake (GL)

RIGHT APPLE

Dark Area . . . . .CRL + RS
Midvalue . . . . . .CO + YO
Light Area . . . . .TYG + YO
Shade . . . . .CRM
                 CRM + DP
Highlight . . . . . .CL + TW
Tint . . . . .BLK + TW
                 CRM + TW

LEFT APPLE

Dark Area . . . . .GL + RS
Midvalue . . . . . .CRL + RS
Light Area . . . . .YO + CO
Shade . . . . .GL + DP
Highlight . . . . . .CRM + TW
Tint . . . . .CL + TYG
                 BLK + TW

BOTTOM CENTER PLUM

Base . . . . .BLK + DP + small amount PB
Highlight . . . . . .TW
Tint . . . . .CRM
                 CRL
                 CO

CENTER LEFT PLUM

Base . . . . .BLK + TW + DP + PB (soft violet)
Shade . . . . .DP + BLK + GL
Tint . . . . .CRM
                 CRL
                 CO

UPPER LEFT PLUM

Base . . . . .PB + BLK + DP (dark blue-violet)
Highlight . . . . . .TW + small amount PB
Tint . . . . .CRM
                 CRL
                 CO
Shade . . . . .DP + BLK

PARTIAL LEFT PLUM

Base . . . . .BLK + DP + GL (deep red-violet)
Highlight . . . . . .CRM
                 TW
Tint . . . . .CRM
                 CRL
                 CO

LOWER RIGHT PLUM

Base . . . . .BLK + TW + DP + PB (midtone
                 blue-violet)
Shade . . . . .CRM + DP + small amount BLK
Tint . . . . .CRM
                 CRL
                 CO
Highlight . . . . . .TW + BLK

LEAVES

Base . . . . .BLK + TW + CL
Shade . . . . .Base mix + BLK
Highlight . . . . . .CL + TW
                 TW
Tint . . . . .YO
                 GL + RS

BRANCHES

Base . . . . .RS
Shade . . . . .BLK
Highlight . . . . . .CL + TW
                 CL + TYG

All remaining plums are painted using the various setups already given. Just balance your colors so that not all of the blue or red plums are clustered together. After completing the painting and placing a coat of varnish on the surface, antique behind the design with CRL + RS. Flyspeck with RS. When applying the tints using the CRM/CRL/CO combination, use the colors in the order listed to form the glints used on the reflected-light areas of the plums. Make each successive application of color slightly smaller than the last color used, and then add a final bright glint of CO.

Plum Country

December 1983

SUNDAY	MONDAY	TUESDAY	WEDNESDAY	THURSDAY	FRIDAY	SATURDAY
		Do what you can, where you are, with what you have.		1	2	3
4	5	6	7	8		

NOVEMBER
1 2 3 4 5
6 7 8 9 10 11 12
13 14 15 16 17 18 19
20 21 22 23 24 25 26
27 28 29 30

JANUARY
1 2 3 4 5 6 7
8 9 10 11 12 13 14
15 16 17 18 19 20 21
22 23 24 25 26 27 28
29 30 31

Plum Delightful

BACKGROUND PREPARATION

Seal the surface with Designs From the Heart wood sealer, and sand when dry. The background for this calendar was painted with Delta Wedgewood Green. The soft, mottled background behind the plums was applied after the painting was completed.

PALETTE

Winsor & Newton Alkyd or Oil Colors:
Ivory Black (BLK), Prussian Blue (PB), Titanium White (TW), Cadmium Orange (CO), Cadmium Yellow Medium (CYM), Cadmium Lemon (CL), Raw Sienna (RS)—oil only

Rembrandt Oil Colors:
Brown Madder Alizarin (BM), Burnt Carmine (BtC)

FULL CENTER PLUM

Dark Area	BLK + small amount PB
Midvalue	BLK + TW
Shade	BLK
Highlight	TW
Tint	CO
	CYM
	BM

TOP CENTER PLUM

Dark Area	BLK + PB + BtC
Light Area	BLK + TW
Shade	BLK
Highlight	TW
Tint	CYM
	BM

LEFT PLUM

Base	BLK + TW
Shade	BLK + PB
	BLK
Tint	BM

RIGHT PLUM

Base	BLK + TW
Shade	BLK
Highlight	TW
Tint	CO
	CYM

LEAVES

Base	BLK + CL + TW
Shade	Dark area mix + BLK
Highlight	BLK + TW
	CL + TW
	TW
Tint	BM
	CO
	CYM

BRANCH

Base	RS
Shade	BLK
Highlight	CL + TW

Use the palette colors to apply the background behind the plums. Start with a dark midvalue mixture of BLK + TW and apply the color behind the leaves, branch and plums at the top of the design. As you swing down to the left, begin to add TW plus some of your leaf green mixtures. Keep the right side a lighter value of gray.

Notice that the yellow-orange tints are on the outer edges of the plums. Where you see CO and CYM listed as a color combination, use the CO first. Apply it to the appropriate areas and blend. Next apply the CYM in a slightly smaller area directly over the CO and blend. You may have to apply the CYM several times for a crisp tint of color. For super sharpness, add highlight glints of CYM in this tint area. Make sure that they are very tiny dots of pure color. The BM has been used mostly in the midvalue area of the plums for a deep burgundy glow. On the top center plum, it appears on the right outside edge and along the lower edge.

Calendar board available from GCP Enterprises, P.O. Box 2104, Claremore, OK 74018-2104. (918) 342-1080.

Plum Delightful

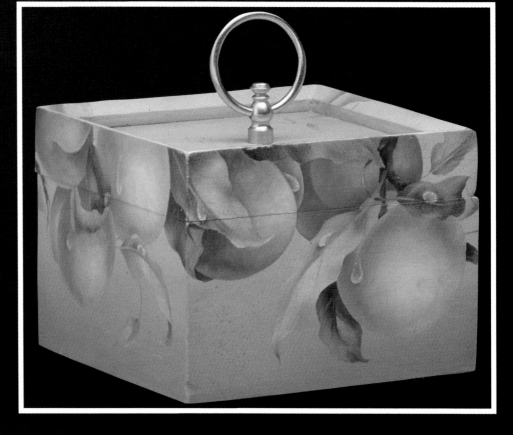

Just Peachy

Just Peachy

BACKGROUND PREPARATION

Seal the surface with Designs From the Heart wood sealer, and sand when dry. The background for this duo of peaches is two parts Accent Antique White and one part Accent Peaches 'N' Cream. Spray-seal with Krylon Matte Finish, no. 1311, and transfer the designs to the surfaces. The lower edge of the filter box was antiqued with CRL + RS + GL. The top surface of the mug rack and the outer edges were antiqued with CRL + RS.

PALETTE

Winsor & Newton Alkyd or Oil Colors:

Cadmium Orange (CO), Cadmium Red Light (CRL), Titanium White (TW), Ivory Black (BLK), Cadmium Lemon (CL), Yellow Ochre (YO), Raw Sienna (RS)—oil only

Grumbacher Oil Colors:

Geranium Lake (GL), Thalo Yellow Green (TYG)

Rembrandt Oil Color:

Naples Yellow Light Extra (NYL)

LIGHTEST PEACHES

Dark Area . . . . .CO + YO + small amount RS

Light Area . . . . .Dark area mix + NYL

Shade . . . . .CRL + RS + small amount GL

Highlight. . . . . .TW

Tint . . . . .BLK + TW TYG (Use only on some of the peaches on box.)

MIDVALUE PEACHES

Dark Area . . . . .RS + CRL

Midvalue . . . . . .YO (Use sparingly.)

Light Area . . . . .Dark area mix + NYL

Shade . . . . .GL + RS

Tint . . . . .CO + NYL CRL + NYL BLK + TW

Highlight. . . . . .TW + CL

DARKEST PEACHES

Base. . . . . .CRL + RS + small amount GL

Shade . . . . .GL + RS

Highlight. . . . . .YO + CO NYL

Tint . . . . .BLK + TW

LIGHTER LEAVES

Base. . . . . .BLK + CL + TW

Shade . . . . .Base mix + BLK

Highlight. . . . . .TW

DARKER LEAVES

Dark Area . . . . .BLK + RS + CL

Light Area . . . . .Dark area mix + CL + TW

Shade . . . . .Dark area mix + BLK

Highlight. . . . . .TW

BRANCHES

Base. . . . . .RS

Shade . . . . .BLK

Highlight. CL

When painting the peaches, keep them soft and coral in color. The light area of the finished peaches should be very close to the background color: This is essential for a soft and delicate look. Remember that the background and the painted objects must relate to each other. Check to see if the peaches have a nice rosy-red look in the dark areas. If they look bruised, you have used too much GL. On the very darkest peaches, you might need to add BU to the shading color to obtain the strongest darks.

Coffee filter box and mug rack available from GCP Enterprises, P.O. Box 2104, Claremore, OK 74018-2104. (918) 342-1080.

Just Peachy

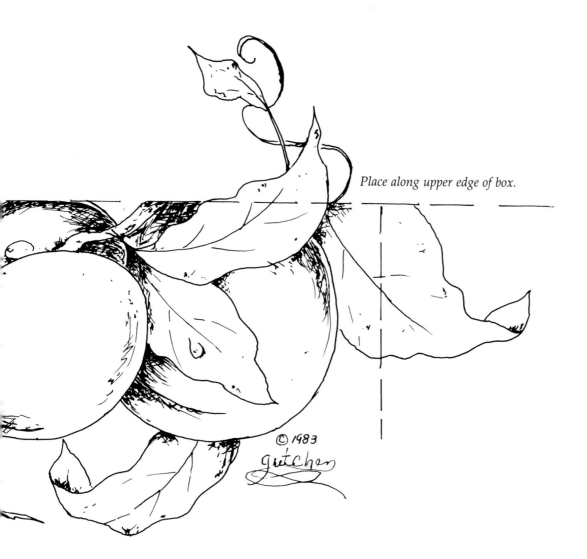

Place along upper edge of box.

© 1983
Gretchen

Place along upper edge of box.

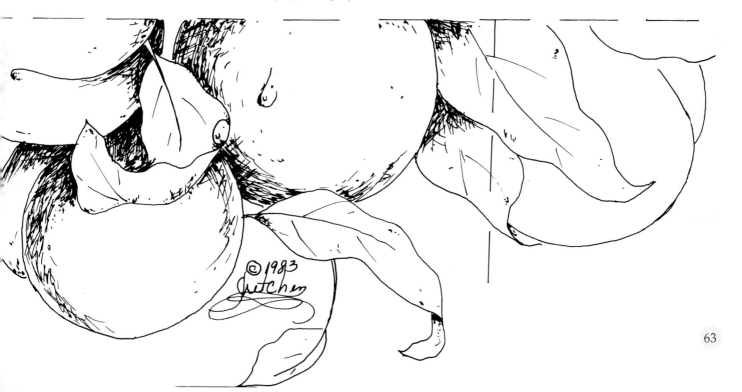

© 1983
Gretchen

63

Summer's Golden Glory

I have painted several of these 9-inch wooden bowls over the years. They are the perfect size for nuts, chips and other such snacks.

BACKGROUND PREPARATION

Seal with Designs From the Heart wood sealer, and sand when dry. Paint the bowl with Delta Antique White. Paint the inset with a mixture of Antique White and Delta Avocado to make a soft yellow-green. Spray with Krylon Matte Finish, no. 1311, and transfer the pattern.

PALETTE

Winsor & Newton Alkyd or Oil Colors:
Cadmium Red Light (CRL), Ivory Black (BLK), Titanium White (TW), Cadmium Lemon (CL), Cadmium Yellow Medium (CYM), Cadmium Orange (CO), Raw Sienna (RS)—oil only

Rembrandt Oil Colors:
Burnt Carmine (BtC), Naples Yellow Hue (NYH), Naples Yellow Light Extra (NYL)

Grumbacher Oil Color:
Geranium Lake (GL)

LIGHTEST APRICOTS

Base . . . . NYH
Dark Area . . . . . BtC
Deepening . . . . . CRL + GL + RS
Add BtC for strongest dark.
Tint . . . . BLK + TW
        CRL + small amount NYH
Highlight . . . . . . CL + TW
        TW

DARKER APRICOTS

Base . . . . CRL + NYH
Dark Area . . . . . BtC
Shade . . . . BtC + BLK
Highlight . . . . . . CYM
        CL
        NYL
Tint . . . . CRL

LEAVES

Dark Area . . . . . BLK + CL
Midvalue . . . . . . CYM
        CO
Light Area . . . . . Dark area mix + BLK
        Dark area mix + GL
Highlight . . . . . . CL + TW
        BLK + TW
Tint . . . . CYM
        CRL
        BtC

LIGHTEST BLOSSOM

Base . . . . NYL
Shade and Tint. RS
        CO
        CRL
        BtC

DARKER BLOSSOMS

Base . . . . NYH + CRL + NYL
Shade . . . . BtC
Highlight . . . . . . NYL
        TW
Tint . . . . CO
        CYM

STEMS

Base . . . . RS
Shade . . . . BLK
Highlight . . . . . . CL + TW

Wooden bowl available from Weston Bowl Mill, P.O. Box 218, Weston, VT 05161-0218. (802) 824-6219.

Summer's Golden Glory

Lemons and Copper

*Lemons
and Copper*

© 1985
[signature]

Patterns for side panels.

Lemons and Copper

BACKGROUND PREPARATION

Seal with Designs From the Heart wood sealer, and sand when dry. Paint the upper panel with Ceramcoat Black acrylic, and stain the remaining areas with BU mixed with odorless brush cleaner. Allow to dry and spray with Krylon Matte Finish, no. 1311, before transferring the pattern. All strokework is executed with the leafy green mixtures from the palette.

PALETTE

Winsor & Newton Alkyd or Oil Colors:

Cadmium Yellow Medium (CYM), Yellow Ochre (YO), Cadmium Lemon (CL), Light Red Oxide (LRO), Ivory Black (BLK), Titanium White (TW), Burnt Umber (BU), Raw Sienna (RS)—oil only.

Grumbacher Oil Color:

Geranium Lake (GL)

LEMONS

Dark Area . . . . .CYM + YO
Midvalue . . . . . .YO + CL
Light Area . . . . .CL + TW
Shade . . . . .Dark area mix
                + BLK
                LRO
Highlight . . . . . .CL + TW
                TW

LEAVES

Dark Area . . . . .BLK + CL
Add RS to some leaves.
Midvalue . . . . . .YO on some
                leaves
Light Area . . . . .CL + BLK +
                TW
Shade . . . . .Dark area mix +
                BLK, or Dark
                area mix + GL
Highlight . . . . . .TW + BLK, or
                CL + TW
                TW

DAISIES

Undercolor . . . .BLK + RS
                YO
Overcolor . . . . .TW + CL
                YO (to dull, if
                necessary)
                TW

DAISY CENTERS

Base . . . . .YO
Shade . . . . .LRO
                BU
Highlight . . . . . .CYM
                CL
                TW

CONTAINER

Dark Area . . . . .RS
Midvalue . . . . . .YO
Light Area . . . . .YO + TW
Shade . . . . .LRO
                LRO + BU
Highlight . . . . . .CL + TW
                TW
Tint . . . . .BLK + TW
                LRO
                CL

Salt box available from GCP Enterprises, P.O. Box 2104, Claremore, OK 74018-2104. (918) 342-1080.

Indian Corn

Indian Corn

BACKGROUND PREPARATION

Seal with Designs From the Heart wood sealer, and sand when dry. Stain the surface with BU paint plus a small amount of odorless brush cleaner. Spray with Krylon Matte Finish, no. 1311. Antique more heavily behind the corn with BU.

PALETTE
Winsor & Newton Alkyd or Oil Colors:

Burnt Umber (BU), Yellow Ochre (YO), Burnt Sienna (BS), Ivory Black (BLK), Cadmium Lemon (CL), Titanium White (TW), Cadmium Yellow Light (CYL), Cadmium Orange (CO), Prussian Blue (PB), Cadmium Red Light (CRL), Dioxazine Purple (DP), Cadmium Yellow Medium (CYM), Raw Sienna (RS)—oil only

Grumbacher Oil Color:
Geranium Lake (GL)

Rembrandt Oil Colors:
Naples Yellow Deep Extra (NYD), Naples Yellow Light Extra (NYL)

CORN HUSKS

Dark Area . . . . .RS
Midvalue . . . . . .YO
Light Area . . . . .NYD
Shade . . . . .BS
              BS + BLK
Highlight . . . . . .CL + TW

CORN
Full Row

Dark Area . . . . .CYL
              CL
Light Area . . . . .TW
Shade . . . . .YO
              RS
              CO

              BS
              BS + PB
              CRL
              GL + DP
Build shading in order to achieve maximum darkness.
Highlight . . . . . .CL + TW
              NYL

First Row Right

Dark Area . . . . .GL + BS
Light Area . . . . .CYL
              CL
              CYM
Shade . . . . .PB + BS
              DP
              BLK
Highlight . . . . . .CL + TW
              NYL

Second Row Right

Dark Area . . . . .GL + BS
Light Area . . . . .PB + BS
              CRL + BS
              CRL + BS +
                CO
Shade . . . . .BLK
              GL + DP
Highlight . . . . . .BLK + PB +
              TW
              CRL
              CO
              CYM
              CL

Third Row Right

Base . . . . .PB + BLK
              GL
              CRL
Shade . . . . .GL + DP
              BLK
Highlight . . . . . .CO
              CYM
              CL
              CRL
              TW

First Row Left

Dark Area . . . . .GL + BS
Light Area . . . . .CRL
Shade . . . . .GL + DP
Highlight . . . . . .CO
              CYM
              CL
              NYL
              TW

Second Row Left

Dark Area . . . . .PB + BS
Light Area . . . . .CRL
              PB + TW +
                small amount
                BLK
Highlight . . . . . .CYM
              CL
              NYL
              TW

STRAWFLOWERS

Red . . . . .CRL
              DP
              CYM
              NYD
Yellow . . . . .CO
              CRL
              GL + DP
              CL
              NYL
Stems . . . . .BU
              NYD
              NYL

RIBBON

Base . . . . .CO
Shade . . . . .CRL
              GL
Highlight . . . . . .CYM

© 1982 Jul Chen

Harvest Fruit

Harvest Fruit

The real glory of autumn is the amber-washed sunsets dappled with crimson and violet, a tapestry of color in perfect harmony. This painting is more challenging than some of the previous projects since it contains multiple elements, each very different from the others, which must be woven into a harmonized unit.

BACKGROUND PREPARATION

Seal with Designs From the Heart wood sealer, and sand when dry. Paint with Delta Cayenne and trim with Delta Barn Red. Spray with Krylon Matte Finish, no. 1311. When finished with the painting, antique along the edges of the surface with AC + BLK.

PALETTE

Winsor & Newton Alkyd Colors:
Cadmium Orange (CO), Cadmium Yellow Medium (CYM), Cadmium Yellow Deep (CYD), Olive Green (OG), Cadmium Lemon (CL), Ivory Black (BLK), Cadmium Red Medium (CRM), Light Red Oxide (LRO), Burnt Umber (BU), Alizarin Crimson (AC), Titanium White (TW), French Ultramarine (FU), Yellow Ochre (YO), Naples Yellow Hue (NYH)

FRONT PUMPKIN

Dark Area . . . . . LRO + CO
Midvalue . . . . . . CO + small amount YO
Light Area . . . . . CYD + small amount NYH
Shade . . . . AC
　　　　　　　　AC + FU
Highlight . . . . . . CYM + NYH
Tint . . . . TW + FU + AC when dry

BACK PUMPKIN

Dark Area . . . . . AC + CO
Light Area . . . . . CO + YO
Shade . . . . OG + AC
Highlight . . . . . . CYM
Tint . . . . TW + FU + AC when dry

FRONT APPLE

Dark Area . . . . . LRO + AC
Midvalue . . . . . . LRO + CRM
Light Area . . . . . CRM
Shade . . . . AC
Highlight . . . . . . CO
　　　　　　　　CRM + TW
Tint . . . . CO + CRM
　　　　　　　　TW + FU + AC when dry

BACK APPLE

Base . . . . LRO + AC
Shade . . . . AC + FU
　　　　　　　　FU
Highlight . . . . . . TW + CRM + LRO
Tint . . . . CO + CRM

PEARS

Base . . . . YO
Shade . . . . OG + small amount AC
Highlight . . . . . . CL + TW
Tint . . . . CRM
　　　　　　　　TW + FU + AC when dry

GRAPES

Base . . . . FU + TW + AC
Shade . . . . FU + AC
Highlight . . . . . . TW
Tint . . . . AC + small amount TW
　　　　　　　　CO + CRM + small amount NYH
　　　　　　　　when dry

STEMS

Base . . . . YO + FU
Shade . . . . FU + AC
Highlight . . . . . . YO + TW

LEAVES

Base . . . . CL + BLK + YO
Shade . . . . Base mix + BLK
Highlight . . . . . . TW
Tint . . . . AC + OG

RESTING AREA

. . . . AC + BU + BLK
. . . . TW + AC + FU
. . . . CRM + CO
Apply the resting area when the painting is dry.

Skill Builders

Plan your painting from background to final tint: Let nothing be done haphazardly or without purpose. Determine the dominant color projected in your painting, and then find ways to use it in each design element. The dominant color in this painting is red-orange, the pumpkin color. To harmonize the entire painting, use a dull, low-key red-orange for the background, and then add a brighter red-orange apple—tint the darker apple, pear and grapes with this color. The blue-violet grapes add an element of coolness to the painting, but they must also be brought into harmony with the other design elements. Never use a color tone on only one element. The cool colors of the grapes are used as reflected lights on the pumpkins, apples and the pear. The crimson apple is brought into harmony by the repetition of its color in the trim and antiquing color of the surface.

Paper towel holder available from Allen's Wood Crafts, 3020 Dogwood Lane, Route 3, Sapulpa, OK 74066. (918) 224-8796.

Step 1—Apply dark, midvalue and light areas to the pumpkins and the lighter apple. Basecoat all remaining elements. The light source is from the upper right; therefore, all elements are light on the upper right and dark on the left side.

On the pumpkins, the front center sections and the sections closer to the light source have the strongest light areas. On the sections to the left, dark areas fall in the overlaps, tapering toward the top, and also form a crescent along the bottom edge and up the left side. As with all crescent forms, they do not touch the outside edge. Apply the midvalue in this area. Even as you are applying paint and beginning to blend, remember the streaks that must be developed.

Step 2—On basecoated elements, add shading in the overlaps and define the crescent shapes on the round objects, leaving reflected light along the dark-side, outside edge. When painting the pear, don't forget the triangular areas of shading that fall in the pinched areas of the neck. Add shading in the pumpkins and the apples, following crescent forms. Allow color to streak into the design elements. Begin the first application of highlight on the pumpkins, apples and the pear.

Step 3—This step develops the strongest shading, highlighting and detail on all design elements. On the front pumpkins, the strongest darks tuck into the triangular overlaps around the apple and grapes. While this side of the pumpkin is closest to the light source, these areas receive less light than the other side because of the overlapping positions of the other elements. Develop stronger highlights on each element, allowing the left pumpkin, left apple and grapes to be the brightest, and thus pulling them closer to your field of vision and into the focal point. Other elements are duller, allowing them to recede further into the background.

Develop final color harmony by tinting each design element with colors from other elements. The pumpkins, front apple and the pear have reflected lights that repeat the blue-violet hues of the grapes. The grapes are tinted along their outer edges with the pumpkin colors. Use these tints where you need to create better separations between the grapes. Adjacent to their darker areas, apply the AC + TW tints. Keep them dark and close to the crescent form. Apply the resting area, remembering to keep the triangular overlapping areas darker in value.

Step 2

Step 1

Step 3

Flowers—

Timeless

Treasures

The Letterholder

Step 1—Base the blossoms with TW + NYH. Shade with YO + CoVH. Base the leaves with TW + CL + BLK. The dark areas of the ribbon should be BLK + TW. Fill in the light areas with TW + NYH.

Step 2—Highlight the blossom with TW. Shade the leaves with the base mixture plus BLK. Shade the ribbon with CoVH + CRD, and tint with TW + BLK + small amounts of CoVH and CRD.

Step 3—Tint the blossom with CRD + CoVH. Use TW to highlight the leaves and ribbon. Finally, add subtle stripes to the outside edges of the ribbon with green leaf mixtures.

The Letterholder

This letterholder with its cutout hearts is a treasure, evoking the feel of Battenberg lace and Victorian times. I've painted it with holly leaves, but you could change them to standard leaves.

BACKGROUND PREPARATION
Apply two coats of White Lightning to the surface.

PALETTE
Winsor & Newton Alkyd or Oil Colors:
Titanium White (TW), Naples Yellow Hue (NYH), Yellow Ochre (YO), Cobalt Violet Hue (CoVH), Cadmium Red Deep (CRD), Cadmium Lemon (CL), Ivory Black (BLK)

BLOSSOMS
Base. . . . . .TW + NYH
Shade . . . . .YO + CoVH
Highlight. . . . . .TW
Tint . . . . .CRD + CoVH

BLOSSOM CENTERS
Dark Area . . . . .CRD + CoVH
Light Area. . . . .TW + CL +
              BLK
Highlight. . . . . .TW
Pollen Dots . . . .TW + NYH

LEAVES
Base. . . . . .TW + CL +
              BLK
Shade . . . . .Base mix + BLK
Highlight. . . . . .TW

BERRIES
Base. . . . . .Values of CRD
              + CoVH +
              TW
Highlight. . . . . .TW

RIBBON

Dark Area . . . . .BLK + TW
Light Area . . . . .TW + NYH
Shade . . . . .CoVH + CRD
Tint . . . . .TW + BLK +
                     small amts.
                     CoVH and
                     CRD
Highlight . . . . . .TW
Stripe . . . . .Green leaf
                     mixtures

Letterholder available from GCP Enterprises,
P.O. Box 2104, Claremore, OK 74018-2104.
(918) 342-1080.

Here's My Heart

BACKGROUND PREPARATION

Seal with Designs From the Heart wood sealer, and sand when dry. Paint the background with a fifty-fifty mixture of Delta Antique White and Mocha. Spray seal with Krylon Matte Finish, no. 1311, and then antique along the upper edges with GL + RS. Transfer the pattern.

PALETTE

Winsor & Newton Alkyd or Oil Colors:

Light Red Oxide (LRO), Dioxazine Purple (DP), Titanium White (TW), Cadmium Yellow Medium (CYM), Cadmium Red Light (CRL), Ivory Black (BLK), Yellow Ochre (YO), Cadmium Lemon (CL), Raw Sienna (RS)—oil only, Naples Yellow Hue (NYH)

Grumbacher Oil Color:

Geranium Lake (GL)

Rembrandt Oil Colors:

Brown Madder Alizarin (BM), Naples Yellow Deep Extra (NYD), Naples Yellow Light Extra (NYL)

LEFT BLOSSOM

Base.........LRO + small
              amount RS
Shade ....DP + BM
Highlight......NYH
              NYD
              NYL
              TW
Tint..........CYM
              CRL
              BLK + TW
              when dry

RIGHT BLOSSOM

Base.........NYD + small
              amount LRO
Shade ....BM
              BM + DP (on
              darkest petals)
Highlight......NYL
              TW
Tint..........CL + NYL
              BLK + TW
              when dry

BLOSSOM CENTERS

Base.........LRO
Shade ....BM + DP
Highlight......CYM + NYD
Tint..........BLK + TW

LEFT DAISY

Undercolor ....LRO + RS
              YO
Overcolor .....NYH + YO +
              CL
Highlight......TW + NYL
Tint..........LRO

Center

Base.........NYL
Shade ....LRO
              BM
Highlight......TW

RIGHT DAISY

Undercolor ....BM
Overcolor .....NYL + CYM +
              YO
Tint..........BM + small
              amount DP

Center

Base.........BM + NYD
Shade ....BM
              BM + DP
Highlight......NYL

FORGET-ME-NOTS

Base.........BLK + TW +
              DP (Vary the
              values from
              dark to light.)
Highlight......TW
Tint..........LRO
              BM
Centers ......LRO
              CYM

LEAVES

Base.........BLK + TW +
            small amount
            CL
Shade ....Base mix + BLK
            + small
            amount CL
Highlight......BLK + TW
Tint ....RS
            Flower colors
Base.........BLK + RS + CL
Shade ....Base mix + BLK
Highlight......TW + CL
            TW

Heart basket available from
GCP Enterprises, P.O.
Box 2104, Claremore,
OK 74018-2104. (918)
342-1080.

©1985
Gretchen

The Bunny Carousel

The Bunny Carousel

© 1987

Even this simple primitive cutout can take on a look of elegance when painted with rich, velvety pansies.

BACKGROUND PREPARATION

Seal with Designs From the Heart wood sealer, and sand when dry. The background for the bunny is painted with Delta Cayenne. The heart and the base are finished with Delta Candy Bar. After spray-sealing with Krylon Matte Finish, no. 1311, antique the joints and the edges of the body and legs with AC + BU. The lighter antiquing on the body is done with TW + BLK. On the base, streak some antiquing with IR. The edges of the heart, the pole and the edges of the base were gold-leafed.

PALETTE
Winsor & Newton Alkyd or Oil Colors:

Burnt Umber (BU), Titanium White (TW), Cadmium Lemon (CL), Cadmium Red Medium (CRM), Indian Red (IR), Ivory Black (BLK), Cadmium Yellow Medium (CYM), Alizarin Crimson (AC), Yellow Ochre (YO), Cadmium Red Light (CRL), Raw Sienna (RS)—oil only

LEFT PANSY

Light Area . . . . . .TW + CL
Dark Area . . . . .TW + CRM + small amount IR
Shade . . . . .IR + AC
        AC + BLK (to form streaks)
Highlight . . . . . . .TW
Tint . . . . .CRL + CYM (in throat)
        TW + BLK
        TW + BLK + AC

Allow the pansy to dry before applying the last two tints. Use only a very small amount of color and gently blend it into the dry surface.

UNDERNEATH LEFT PANSY
Base. . . . . .AC
Shade . . . . .BLK
Highlight. . . . . .TW + BLK

TOP CENTER PANSY
Front Three Petals
Base. . . . . .CL + YO + TW
Highlight. . . . . .TW + CL
Streaks . . . . . . .IR
Deepening
  Streaks . . . . . . IR + AC +
                      BLK
Tint . . . . .CL + CRL (in
                      throat)

Back Two Petals
Base. . . . . .CL + RS
Highlight. . . . . .CL + TW
Shade . . . . .AC + IR
Tint . . . . .AC + BLK +
                      TW
                    IR + AC

Bunny carousel available from GCP Enterprises, P.O. Box 2104, Claremore, OK 74018-2104. (918) 342-1080.

The Bunny Carousel

Light Area   Base

Dark Area

Shade

Streaks

Highlight

Tint

Base

Light Area

Highlight

Dark Area

Tint
Streaks

Highlight
Tint

Base

Shade

Highlight

Tint

Painted in Pink

Painted in Pink

Simple pink and burgundy pansies adorned with elegance dress up a rather plain lingerie chest. This free-flying, multipart pattern can become a painting nightmare if you are unable to create a focal point within the design. There are several main design areas on the chest, and only one can be the primary area of interest.

BACKGROUND PREPARATION

Seal with Designs From the Heart wood sealer, and sand when dry. Paint the drawer fronts, the top and the sides with FolkArt Tapioca. Paint the front of the chest with Ceramcoat Stonewedge Green. Paint all areas to be gold leafed, including the embossed wood trim, with Ceramcoat Red Iron Oxide. Gold leaf the upper crown, the routed edge of the top, the front beaded edge and the pedestal, as well as all embossed wood trim. Spray-seal everything with Krylon Matte Finish, no. 1311. Using a thinned mixture of FT + LRO, apply a rule of paint ½″ from the left, right and bottom side of each drawer. Do the same on the top of the chest. When the painting is completed, attach the embossed wood trim. Lightly antique behind the drawer scrolls, around the side trim and at the crown with LRO + AC.

PALETTE
Winsor & Newton Alkyd Colors:

Flesh Tint (FT), Cadmium Lemon (CL), Light Red Oxide (LRO), Alizarin Crimson (AC), Cadmium Orange (CO), Naples Yellow Hue (NYH), Ivory Black (BLK), Burnt Umber (BU), Titanium White (TW), Cadmium Red Light (CRL)

PINK PANSY

Light Streaks . . .CL
Base. . . . . .FT
Shade . . . . .LRO + AC
Tint . . . . .CL + NYH
Highlight. . . . . .TW
Dark Streaks . . .LRO + AC + BU
Tint . . . . .TW + BLK when dry

BURGUNDY PANSY

Light Streaks . . .CO
Base. . . . . .AC + LRO
Shade . . . . .AC + BU
Highlight. . . . . .CRL
                    CO
                    FT
                    TW
Dark Streaks . . .BU + AC
Tint . . . . .TW + BLK

LEAVES

Base. . . . . .TW + BLK + CL
Shade . . . . .Base mix + BLK
                    CL may be added if the shading is
                       too dull.
Highlight. . . . . .TW
Tint . . . . .Flower colors

Lingerie chest and embossed wood trim are available from GCP Enterprises, P.O. Box 2104, Claremore, OK 74018-2104. (918) 342-1080.

95

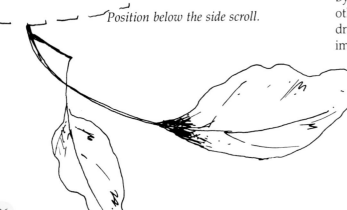

Position above the side scroll.

Skill Builders

Three elements are essential in creating the focal point of a design: color, contrast and detail. All elements must be included in one central area in order to draw the viewer's attention. Concentrate them in several areas and the viewer becomes confused, because you've created more than one focal area. Spread the elements too far apart within a design area, and you have no focal point. While this design has many design areas, only one is an attention getter.

I have chosen to create the focal point at the center of the pansy design, where the two pansies overlap one another. Let's look at each element to see the role it plays in developing this focal point.

COLOR

Within the focal area, I have used complementary colors immediately next to each other. Complementary colors are two colors that are opposite each other on the color wheel. When used side by side, each color seems brighter, and will draw the eye into that area of the design. It is an instant attention getter. The pansies fall into the red family of colors, and they are surrounded by green leaves. Red and green are complementary colors.

CONTRAST

By painting one of the pansies very dark in value and the other very light, I have created a visual difference that draws attention. The painting would not have the same impact if both pansies were light pink or burgundy. On

Position below the side scroll.

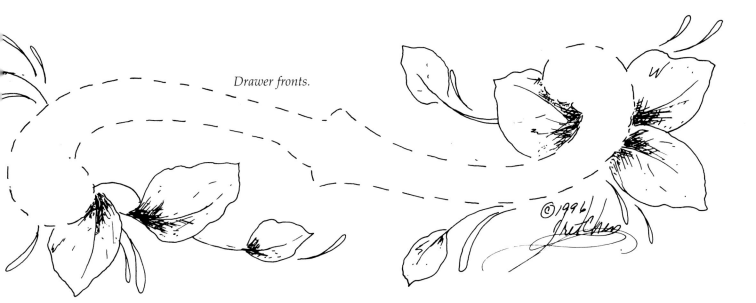

Drawer fronts.

© 1996

the pink pansy, I have created very strong, dark streaks and shadow areas that are contrasted with strong highlights and the lighter color of the blossom. The red pansy has less contrast within the flower, so it does not command as much individual attention. Other pansies within the design have less contrast within their petals.

DETAIL

Detail includes pansy streaks, waterdrops, position of tendrils, and flips and turns on flower and leaf edges.

On the pink pansy, I was very careful to create strong, well-defined streaks. While the burgundy pansy is streaked, it is not as obvious, since there is less contrast between the streaks and the basic flower color. Only on the pink pansy did I create flips on the petal edges. Notice how the leaves around this central design core are also curled, flipped and tinted with pansy color. Position tendrils carefully. Always allow the ends to turn to the focal point, leading the viewer to look more closely at this area. The final touch is the waterdrops. Their sparkle will catch all the attention. Cluster them around the focal point rather than sprinkling them throughout the design.

Top of chest.

© 1996

97

On the pink pansy, block in the yellow streaks and base all areas except for the dark streaked area. Add soft tints into the three front petals and apply shading into all overlaps. Blend shading so that it begins to follow the growth pattern. On the burgundy pansy, apply the light streaks, base the remainder of the flower petals and apply shading in the overlaps.

Waterdrops are easy on a wet surface. If the final look doesn't please you, blend them out and start again.

Scratch out the shape of the drop with a stylus. Load a no. 2 flat brush with white paint, and paint an elongated C stroke. Stand the brush on the chisel edge at the long side. Pull down, applying pressure as the drop fattens. Let up on the pressure, allowing the brush to come back to the chisel edge on the short side. Blend inside the drop, leaving the strongest color in the fattest portion. If necessary, strengthen the color. If painting the drop on a light color, it may be necessary to add some darker subject-matter color into the opening at the top. Anchor the drop with a darker value of the subject-matter color and blend into the subject. Complete the drop with bright highlight glints. Add a dot and a broken dash in the opening on the short side, and a dot in the fat bottom portion.

98

On the pink pansy, apply strong streaks to the three front petals. Stand the brush on the chisel edge and pull from the center, fanning outward into the petal. Allow the streaks to be longer at the sides and shorter at the center area. Apply softer and less detailed streaks on the other petals. On the burgundy pansy, continue to build the highlight lighter in value, and apply the streaks.

On the pink pansy, strengthen the shaded areas and apply the highlights. On the burgundy pansy, apply the first application of highlight color and strengthen shaded areas where necessary.

On the pink pansy, strengthen and enhance the streaks, dark areas and highlights. Add the TW + BLK tints. On the burgundy pansy, apply the final highlight color and tint. Strengthen dark areas and streaks where necessary.

The Presence of Poppies

Poppies, like daisies, are an ever-present favorite and staple of decorative painters. Like daisies, they also come in every imaginable color. The soft, peachy tones of this painting make it one of my favorites. I love the soothing quality of this soft, delicate tint of color. Place me in a peachy environment and give me a fresh peach shake to drink, and I think I'm getting pretty close to heaven.

BACKGROUND PREPARATION

Seal with Designs From the Heart wood sealer, and sand when dry. Paint with Ceramcoat Dunes Beige. Apply copper leaf, following the manufacturer's directions, along the outer perimeter of the painting surface. Spray the entire box with Krylon Matte Finish, no. 1311. When the painting is finished, antique and flyspeck along the lower edges of the sides of the box with TW + FT + small amount of LRO. Antique the corners of the painting surface with the same color. Lighten the antiquing mix by adding more TW and NYH, and apply between the upper ribbon section and the poppy.

PALETTE

Winsor & Newton Alkyd Colors:
Flesh Tint (FT), Titanium White (TW), Naples Yellow Hue (NYH), Alizarin Crimson (AC), Cadmium Orange (CO), Cadmium Lemon (CL), Light Red Oxide (LRO), Cobalt Violet Hue (CoVH), Ivory Black (BLK)

POPPY

Base	TW + FT
Shade	Base mix + LRO
	LRO + AC
Highlight	TW
Tint	TW + CO
	TW + BLK + CoVH
Streaks	CoVH + BLK when dry

POPPY CENTER

Base	BLK
Highlight	TW + AC
Pollen	AC + TW + LRO
	AC + BLK

RIBBON

Base	TW + NYH
Shade	Base mix + BLK
Highlight	TW
Tint	Poppy colors
Stripe	CoVH + LRO

LEAVES

Base	TW + CL + BLK
Shade	Base mix + BLK
	Add AC to the darkest leaf.
Highlight	TW
Tint	Poppy colors

Skill Builders

Learning to balance cool and warm colors and bright and dull colors within a design will help to create dimension and drama in your painting. Cool and/or dull colors will cause an area of the design to recede, while the use of bright, intense and/or warm colors will cause an area of the design to come forward. Not only these elements will be used to create the dimension of the poppy: We will also draw on some of the rules used to create dimension on round objects.

The Presence of Poppies

continued from page 101.

The front center petal cupping over the poppy center is treated as a round object. The darker colors do not touch the outside edge of the object, and they form a modified crescent following the shape of the petal. The reflected-light area behind the crescent will be midvalue in color and, like most fruits, will be tinted with a dull, cool gray color, causing this area to recede away from your field of vision and wrap toward the poppy center.

The same cool gray tints are placed along the outer edges of the petals closest to the stem. These petals arch away, and then the tips roll under. To create this illusion, place a bright, intense highlight at the center of the petal, and tint the receding edges with the cool, dull gray tint. The same tint can be used in an underlap adjacent to the shading.

Use warm tints, such as CO + TW, where an area of the design must come forward. Strong orange tints are used on all the remaining petals, since none of them have receding, rolled edges. Warm tints should be positioned in the midvalue area of the design close to the light and highlighted areas. Place them near a shaded area and the painting looks strained and out of balance.

Build the strongest, brightest, most intense highlights on the highest arches of the petals. The strongest highlight is laid adjacent to the poppy center, helping to draw attention to this area of the design. Apply less intense highlights to the other arched areas.

102

Carefully trace the pattern and base the areas where pleats and folds are formed. If necessary, lay your tracing over the area and, using a stylus, accurately retrace the pleat and fold. The outside line forming along the left side of the inner fold should be parallel to the line forming on the front of the fold. If that line points to the left, the painting will be out of perspective. Apply darker color in each overlapping area, and highlight to the top of the pleat and along the top of the fold.

Base the poppy with a warm pink. This warmer color will allow the flower to come forward, away from the background. Apply shading in each of the overlaps and where the petals ripple downward. Leave a scant amount of reflected light along the front center petal.

Strengthen all shadow areas with a cool color, and add the warm orange tints in areas that project forward. Begin to build the highlights. Dab in the brighter and more intense streak color along the bowl, remembering to leave the area of reflected light. Apply some of the same color above the flower center.

Strengthen all highlights, shading and warm tints, if necessary. Pull streaks using the chisel of the flat brush. Add the cooler, duller gray tints to the receding areas.

103

Spring Medley

BACKGROUND PREPARATION

Seal with Designs From the Heart wood sealer, and sand when dry. Paint with DecoArt Flesh. Spray-seal with Krylon Matte Finish, no. 1311, and transfer the patterns.

PALETTE

Winsor & Newton Alkyd or Oil Colors:

Cadmium Red Light (CRL), Yellow Ochre (YO), Alizarin Crimson (AC), Titanium White (TW), Ivory Black (BLK), Cadmium Lemon (CL), Naples Yellow Hue (NYH), French Ultramarine (FU), Cadmium Orange (CO), Cadmium Yellow Deep (CYD)

TULIPS

Antiquing Around Tulips

CRL + YO + AC
YO

Upper Right Tulip

Base	TW + NYH
Shade	NYH + CRL
	CRL + small amount AC
Highlight	TW
Tint	TW + BLK
	TW + CL

Center Left Tulip

Dark Area	CRL + YO + AC
Light Area	CRL + NYH + TW
Shade	AC + YO
Highlight	NYH + TW
	TW
Tint	CL
	BLK + TW

Center Right Tulip

Dark Area	CRL + NYH
Light Area	NYH + TW
Shade	CRL + YO + AC
Highlight	TW
Tint	TW + BLK
	TW + CRL

Lower Tulip Bud

Same as center left tulip, but add more TW.

Tulip Leaves

Base	TW + CL + BLK
Shade	Base mix + CL + BLK
Highlight	TW
Tint	Flower colors
	TW + BLK
	TW + FU + BLK

Tulip Ribbon

Dark Area	CRL + TW + YO
Midvalue	CRL + NYH
Light Area	NYH + TW
Shade	CRL + YO + small amount AC
Highlight	TW
Tint	CO
	TW + BLK

NARCISSUS

Antiquing Around Narcissus

CRL + YO + TW
YO

Trumpets

Base	CRL + TW + YO
Highlight	CL + TW
Shade	AC + YO + small amount CRL
Tint	CO

Outer Petals

Base	TW + NYH
Shade	TW + BLK + small amount FU
Highlight	TW
Tint	CYD
	TW + BLK

Narcissus Leaves

Base	TW + CL + BLK
Shade	Base mix + CL + BLK
Highlight	TW + small amount CL
	TW
Tint	CO
	CRL + TW + YO

Narcissus Ribbon

Dark Area	CRL + YO
Light Area	CRL + NYH + TW
Shade	YO + AC
Highlight	NYH + TW + small amount CL
	TW
Tint	TW + FU + BLK

Surfaces available from GCP Enterprises, P.O. Box 2104, Claremore, OK 74018-2104. (918) 342-1080.

Spring Medley

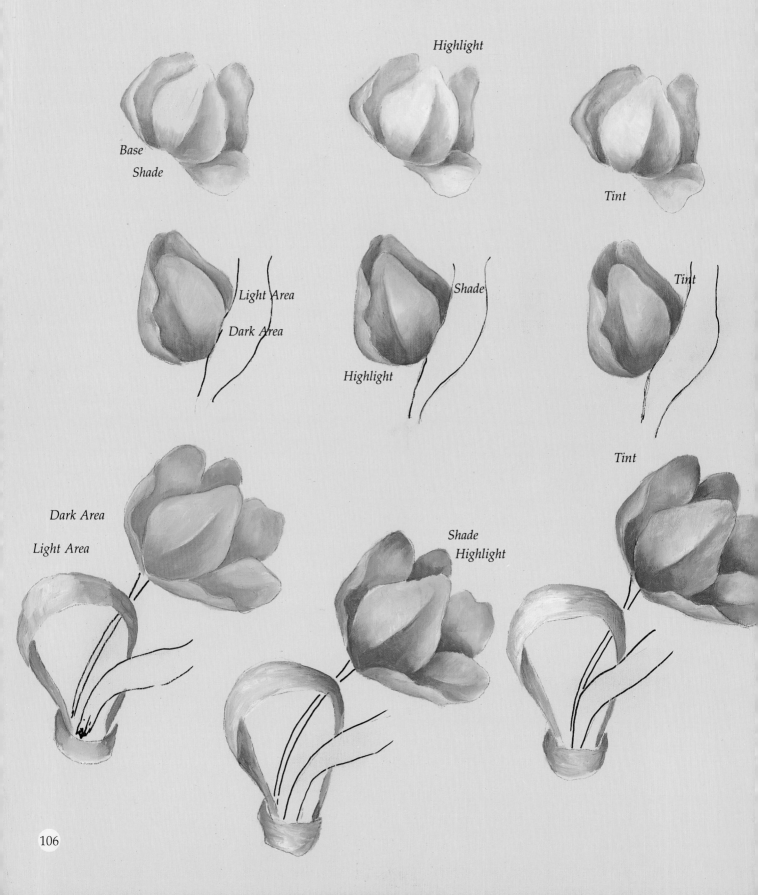

Highlight

Base
Shade

Tint

Light Area

Dark Area

Shade

Highlight

Tint

Tint

Dark Area

Light Area

Shade
Highlight

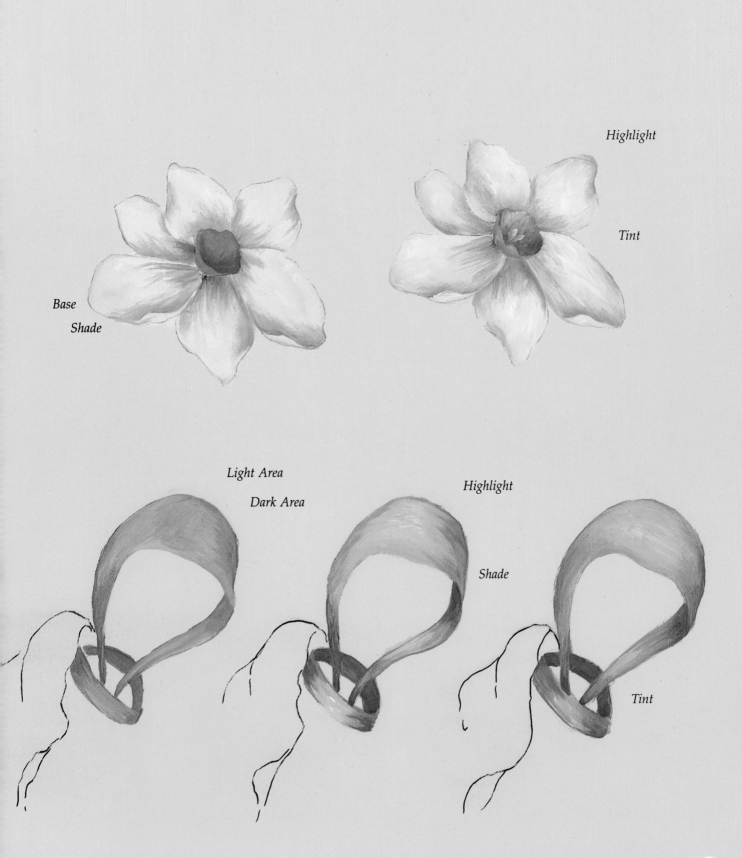

Highlight

Tint

Base

Shade

Light Area

Dark Area

Highlight

Shade

Tint

Spring Medley

Tulips

Narcissus

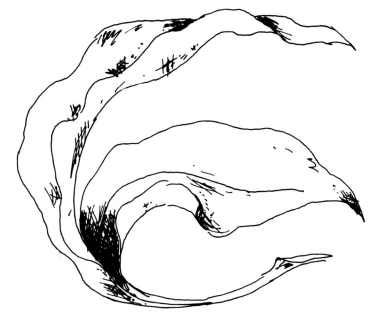

Reverse this pattern and apply it to the top of the shelf on the right side.

Late February arrives and a softer, gentler day of warmth brings thoughts of spring and the floral glory that accompanies the season. Tulips, among the first of Nature's summons of the coming season, brighten up the flower-beds and my spirit.

BACKGROUND PREPARATION

Seal with Designs From the Heart wood sealer and sand. Paint the shelf with Americana Taupe and spray with Krylon Matte Finish, no. 1311. Lightly transfer the pattern with gray graphite paper.

Apply the sponged trim using a natural sea sponge moistened with water. Pick up a small amount of white acrylic paint and blot on the palette to eliminate the excess; check the density of color. It should be soft and transparent. Softly tap the sponge against the surface, leaving a soft white accent. If the color becomes too heavy and the background is no longer visible, clean the sponge in water, wring out excess moisture, reload with the background color, blot on the palette and tap on the surface until the white is subdued.

PALETTE
Winsor & Newton Alkyd Colors:
Dioxazine Purple (DP), Cadmium Lemon (CL), Cadmium Red Deep (CRD), Ivory Black (BLK), Titanium White (TW), Naples Yellow Hue (NYH)

Springtime Delicacy

TULIPS
Base . . . . TW + NYH
Shade . . . . Base mix + small amount BLK
Highlight . . . . . . TW
Tint . . . . TW + CL + BLK
Accent . . . . DP + CRD

LEAVES AND STEMS
Base . . . . TW + CL + BLK
Shade . . . . Base mix + BLK
Highlight . . . . . . TW
Tint . . . . TW + DP + CRD + BLK

The brightness and intensity of the white highlight sets the color tone for the flower, and also creates the fuller contour of the blossom. Bright, intense color will cause an area of the design to come forward. To make an area recede, use duller, more grayed colors, especially within the shadow areas.

Shelf available from GCP Enterprises, P.O. Box 2104, Claremore, OK 74018-2104. (918) 342-1080.

Skill Builders

Painting a white object can present some challenges. Look at any white flower and you will find that it is really many different shades of white. When painting a white object, the whiteness is projected in the highlight. Begin by basing the white element with a dull off-white rather than pure white.

© 1996
Gretchen

Step 1—Basecoat the tulip and leaves. Using the handle of the paintbrush, scratch out the petal separations and folds.

Step 2—The front, center petal of the tulip has the same shape and form as a leaf; therefore, place shading in all the same positions. When applying shading to the back petals, be sure to apply stronger dark color in the triangular corners.

Step 3—Build strong white highlights on the tulip. The center vein area of the front center petal may require several applications of highlight. This petal also has a soft yellow-green tint placed in the midvalue area. Tints are normally midvalue in color and are positioned within the midvalue area of the element.

Step 4—Strengthen all highlights and shading, if necessary. The tints on the leaves and the accents along the tulip edges introduce the background color into the painting, thus creating color harmony throughout. To accent the center petal, splotch color along the petal edge and pull with the growth pattern in a streaky motion. Soften and blend the accents on the other petals. The stronger detail on the front petal creates a focal point for the design.

113

Heart of Spring

Heart of Spring

BACKGROUND PREPARATION

Seal with Designs From the Heart wood sealer, and sand when dry. Paint the front and back of the surface with Delta Indiana Rose acrylic. Paint the trim on the upper right and along the sides with Delta Coral acrylic. Spray with Krylon Matte Finish, no. 1311, and transfer the pattern.

PALETTE

Winsor & Newton Alkyd or Oil Colors:
Ivory Black (BLK), Titanium White (TW), Yellow Ochre (YO), Cadmium Lemon (CL), Light Red Oxide (LRO), Raw Sienna (RS)—oil only.

Rembrandt Oil Colors:
Naples Yellow Deep Extra (NYD), Naples Yellow Light Extra (NYL)

Grumbacher Oil Colors:
Geranium Lake (GL), Thalo Yellow Green (TYG)

LIGHT TULIP

Dark	NYD + TYG
Light	NYL
Shade	Dark mix + BLK + small amount LRO
Highlight	TW
Tint	LRO + NYL BLK + TW

DARK TULIP

Dark	GL + LRO
Midvalue	NYD
Light	NYL
Shade	GL + BLK
Highlight	NYL + TW TW
Tint	BLK + TW NYD

MIDVALUE TULIP

Light	NYL
Dark	NYL + LRO
Shade	LRO
Highlight	TW

TULIP CENTERS

Base	BLK + RS
Highlight	NYD TW

DOGWOOD BLOSSOMS

Base	NYL
Shade	YO + BLK BLK + TW
Highlight	TW
Tint	LRO + GL + small amount BLK TYG BLK + TW YO

DOGWOOD CENTERS

Base	BLK + CL
Circles	Base mix + CL + TW

PUSSY WILLOWS

Base	BLK + TW
Shade	BLK
Tint	Pink mixtures
Line Work	TW TW + BLK

PUSSY WILLOW STEMS

Base	RS + TW
Shade	BLK

LEAVES

Base	BLK + CL + TW
Shade	BLK + RS
Highlight	TW
Tint	LRO + GL RS Pink mixtures

STROKEWORK AND LINE WORK

Dark pink mixtures

Heart surface available from GCP Enterprises, P.O. Box 2104, Claremore, OK 74018-2104. (918) 342-1080.

Summer Glory

Base

Shade

Highlight

Stripes

Tint

Summer Glory

BACKGROUND PREPARATION

Seal wood with Designs From the Heart wood sealer, and sand when dry. Paint with off-white acrylic paint. Spray seal with Krylon Matte Finish, no. 1311. No preparation is required for the porcelain hummingbird and box.

PALETTE
Winsor & Newton Alkyd or Oil Colors:

Titanium White (TW), Naples Yellow Hue (NYH), Cadmium Red Deep (CRD), Sap Green (SG), Cadmium Lemon (CL), French Ultramarine (FU), Ivory Black (BLK), Dioxazine Purple (DP)

MORNING GLORIES

Base	TW + NYH
Shade	CRD + DP
Highlight	TW
Stripes	SG + CL + TW
Deepening	CRD + DP
Tints	TW + FU + BLK
	SG + CL

LEFT CENTER FLOWER

Apply more NYH on the trumpet and add a strong tint of SG + CL. There is only a small amount of shading along the lower edge.

RIGHT CENTER FLOWER

This flower has very little NYH, but is strongly tinted with TW + FU + BLK. Be sure that each stripe has a bit of shading along either side.

LEAVES

Base	CL + BLK + TW
Shade	Base mix + BLK + FU
Highlight	TW
Tint	FU + TW
	CRD + DP

BACKGROUND

Fill in with various mixtures of TW + DP + BLK + FU, keeping the color darker around the flowers and lighter as you extend toward the top of the frame.

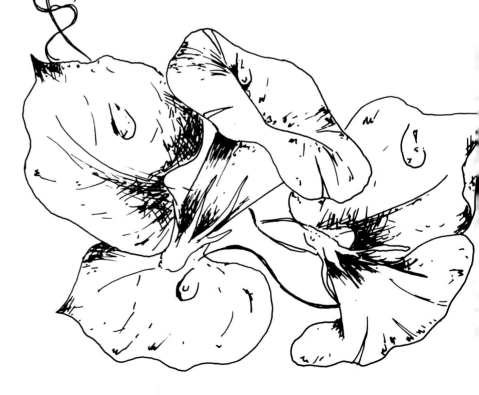

Top of box.

PORCELAIN HUMMINGBIRD

Stain the bird, with the exception of the breast and throat, with a mixture of SG + odorless brush cleaner. Allow to dry, and then add a touch of CRD + DP to the throat. Shade under the tail and the wings with a scant amount of DP. Softly blend with an old brush. Add a scant amount of DP to the overlaps on the top of the tail and the wings. Stain the beak with DP + BLK. Paint the eyes with BLK and glint with TW.

PORCELAIN BOX

Paint the lower edge of the bottom and the outer edge of the top with TW + FU + BLK. On the bottom of the box, paint TW at the top and blend with the darker color. The inset on the top of the box is painted with the background colors. Paint the flowers similar to those on the frame. The strokework is painted with gold metallic acrylic paint.

All surfaces available from GCP Enterprises, P.O. Box 2104, Claremore, OK 74108-2104. (918) 342-1080.

In northeastern Oklahoma, where I live, the grapes begin to ripen in mid-August. Rich in color and frosted with Nature's waxy preservative, they are a painter's joy.

This little box, a silverware chest that stores flatware in an upright position, is enhanced with a bounty of grapes in both blue and red, each accented with the colors from the other. The single poppy knits the design elements together, with a profusion of soft coral tones accented with the grape colors.

BACKGROUND PREPARATION

Seal with Designs From the Heart wood sealer, and sand when dry. Basecoat the lid with Accent Country Colors Brick. Allow to dry, and then spray with Krylon Matte Finish, no. 1311. The lower portion of the box is painted using Ceramcoat Dusty Mauve. When dry, wet this area with DecoArt Control Medium and use a natural, large-hole sea sponge to lightly sponge Americana Ultra Blue, Ultra Blue + any off-white, Ceramcoat Deep Coral and Ceramcoat Golden Brown. When complete, copper leaf the edge of the lid and a 1-inch-wide band around the box, 1 inch up from the bottom.

PALETTE
Winsor & Newton Alkyd Colors:
Titanium White (TW), Ivory Black (BLK), Light Red Oxide (LRO), French Ultramarine (FU), Cadmium Lemon (CL), Naples Yellow Hue (NYH), Alizarin Crimson (AC), Cobalt Violet Hue (CoVH)

BLOSSOM
Base	LRO + NYH
Shade	LRO + AC
	AC + BLK
Highlight	TW + NYH
	TW
Pollen	BLK
	AC
Tint	AC + CoVH + TW + BLK
	TW + FU + CoVH + BLK

(Use various mixtures.)

FLOWER CENTER
Base	TW + CoVH + BLK
Shade	Base mix + BLK + CoVH
Highlight	LRO + NYH + small amount AC + TW

Apply all basecoats and shading.

LEAVES

Base . . . . TW + BLK +
                  CL
Shade . . . . Base mix + BLK
                  Shade mix + AC
                  + BLK +
                  CoVH
Highlight . . . . . . TW + CL
                  TW
Tint . . . . Flower and
                  grape mixtures

Silverware box available from GCP Enterprises, P.O. Box 2104, Claremore, OK 74018-
2104. (918) 342-1080.

Apply deeper shade values and highlights.

RIBBON

Base . . . . LRO + small
                  amount NYH
Shade . . . . CoVH
                  CoVH + BLK
Highlight . . . . . . TW + AC
Tint . . . . TW + FU
Stripe . . . . CoVH + TW +
                  small amount
                  BLK

RED GRAPES

Base . . . . AC + LRO
Shade . . . . AC + FU +
                  BLK
Highlight . . . . . . TW + NYH
                  TW
Tint . . . . TW + AC
Glints . . . . Same as Tint

BLUE GRAPES

Base . . . . AC + FU + TW
                  + small
                  amount BLK
Shade . . . . FU + BLK
Highlight . . . . . . TW + NYH
Tint . . . . TW + FU
                  AC + TW
Glints . . . . Same as Tint

Strengthen shading and highlights, and add tints.

Golden Treasure

BACKGROUND PREPARATION

The background for this lovely clock is unusual and interesting. After sealing with Designs From the Heart wood sealer and sanding, paint the entire surface with Ceramcoat Butter Yellow acrylic. Spray-seal with Krylon Matte Finish, no. 1311, then antique the right side with TW oil paint. The upper left and lower edge of the clock are antiqued with RS. Flyspeck with RS.

PALETTE

Winsor & Newton Alkyd or Oil Colors:

Olive Green (OG), Yellow Ochre (YO), Titanium White (TW), Cadmium Lemon (CL), Burnt Umber (BU), Cadmium Yellow Medium (CYM), Raw Sienna (RS)—oil only

Rembrandt Oil Colors:

Naples Yellow Light Extra (NYL), Naples Yellow Deep Extra (NYD)

BLOSSOMS

Base	NYL
Shade	OG + YO
Highlight	TW
Tint	RS
	YO
	NYD

CENTERS

Base	YO
Shade	RS
Highlight	CL + NYL
	TW
Linework	BU
Dots	NYL
	YO

LEAVES

Dark Area	OG + RS
Midvalue	YO
Light Area	Dark area mix + CL + NYL
Shade	Dark area mix + BU
Highlight	CL + TW
	TW
Tint	CYM
	BU

BERRIES, LIGHT LEAVES, BRANCHES AND STEMS

Base	OG + small amount TW
Highlight	TW
Shade	RS on berries only

Clock available from GCP Enterprises, P.O. Box 2104, Claremore, OK 74018-2104. (918) 342-1080.

Apricot Frost

Apricot Frost

BACKGROUND PREPARATION

Seal with Designs From the Heart wood sealer and sand when dry. Paint with Accent Country Colors Peaches 'N' Cream, and trim with Delta Fleshtone. Spray seal with Krylon Matte Finish, no. 1311. Antique on the color break with TOR.

PALETTE

Winsor & Newton Alkyd or Oil Colors:

Cadmium Orange (CO), Cadmium Red Light (CRL), Titanium White (TW), Ivory Black (BLK), Dioxazine Purple (DP), Yellow Ochre (YO), Cadmium Lemon (CL)

Rembrandt Oil Colors:

Transparent Oxide Red (TOR), Naples Yellow Light Extra (NYL), Naples Yellow Deep Extra (NYD)

Grumbacher Oil Color:

Geranium Lake (GL)

LIGHT BLOSSOM

Base . . . . .NYL + CO + CRL (similar to background)
Shade . . . . .CRL + TOR
Highlight . . . . . .TW
Tint . . . . .CRL
BLK + TW

DARK BLOSSOM

Dark Area . . . . .TOR + small amount GL
Midvalue . . . . . .CRL
Light Area . . . . .NYL + CO + CRL
Shade . . . . .GL + DP
Highlight . . . . . .NYL + CL TW
Tint . . . . .BLK + TW

BLOSSOM CENTERS

Base . . . . .CRL + YO
Shade . . . . .TOR
Highlight . . . . . .CL + NYL
Splotches . . . . . .NYL
CL + NYL
CRL + NYL

LIGHT TULIPS

Base . . . . .NYD
Shade . . . . .CRL + YO
        TOR
Highlight . . . . . .CL + NYL
        TW
Tint . . . . .BLK + TW

DARK TULIP

Base . . . . .CRL + NYL +
        CO
Shade . . . . .CRL + GL
        TOR
Highlight . . . . . .NYD
        NYL
Tint . . . . .BLK + TW

TULIP LEAVES

Base . . . . .BLK + CL +
        TW (pale gray-
        green)
Shade . . . . .Base mix + BLK
Highlight . . . . . .TW + small
        amount CL
Tint . . . . .TOR

BLOSSOM LEAVES

Dark Area . . . . .BLK + CL +
        small amount
        RS
Midvalue . . . . . .TOR, or YO
Light Area . . . . .Dark area mix +
        CL + TW
Shade . . . . .Dark area mix +
        BLK
Add TOR to some leaves.

Highlight . . . . . .BLK + TW, or
        CL + TW
        TW
Tint . . . . .Red mixtures
        BLK + TW

FILLER FLOWERS

TOR
NYD
NYL + CL
TW
Green mixtures

Use colors in order listed. Thin
with linseed oil to keep them soft and
delicate.

Surfaces available from Designs by Bentwood,
Inc., P.O. Box 1676, Thomasville, GA 31799-
1676. (912) 226-1223.

©1984

© 1984
Gretchen

Apricot Frost

Celine's Poppies

Celine's Poppies

This stationery box was designed and painted for a dear friend, Celine Yelverton. Her encouraging words and kind remarks have been a continuing inspiration to me and other painting friends.

BACKGROUND PREPARATION

Apply a coat of White Lightning to the surface, and spray with Krylon Matte Finish, no. 1311. Trace the pattern on, and then rub CRL + RS and CO + YO in and around the flowers for a soft, shadowy effect. Also apply some of this to the outer edges of the lid. The trim and inside of the box are done with Delta Terra Cotta, and then antiqued with GL + RS. Follow up with flyspecks of the same color.

PALETTE

Winsor & Newton Alkyd or Oil Colors:

Cadmium Orange (CO), Yellow Ochre (YO), Cadmium Lemon (CL), Titanium White (TW), Cadmium Red Light (CRL), Dioxazine Purple (DP), Ivory Black (BLK), Raw Sienna (RS)—oil only

Rembrandt Oil Colors:

Brown Madder Alizarin (BM), Naples Yellow Light Extra (NYL)

LIGHT ORANGE POPPY

Dark Area . . . . .BM + RS
Midvalue . . . . . .CO + YO
Light Area . . . . .CL + YO
Shade . . . . .BM + RS
Highlight . . . . . .NYL
                     TW

RED-ORANGE POPPY

Dark Area . . . . .BM + RS
Midvalue . . . . . .CRL + RS
Light Area . . . . .YO + CO
Shade . . . . .BM + DP
Highlight . . . . . .NYL
                     TW

DEEP RED POPPY

Base . . . . .BM + RS
Shade . . . . .BM + DP
Highlight . . . . . .CRL + RS
                     CO + YO

POPPY CENTER

Base . . . . .BLK + small
                     amount CL
Highlight . . . . . .CL + TW
                     TW
Splotches . . . . . .BLK + CL

BUDS

Dark Area . . . . .BLK + CL
Light Area . . . . .CO + YO
Shade . . . . .Dark area mix +
                     BLK
Tint CL
                     CRL + RS
                     CO

DARKEST LEAVES

Dark Area . . . . .BLK + CL
Light Area . . . . .Dark area mix +
                     CL + TW
Shade . . . . .Dark area mix +
                     BLK, or Dark
                     area mix + CL
Highlight . . . . . .CL + TW
                     TW
Tint . . . . .Flower colors

LIGHTEST LEAVES

Base . . . . .BLK + CL +
                     TW
Highlight . . . . . .TW
Tint . . . . .YO
                     RS

Box available from GCP Enterprises, P.O. Box
2104, Claremore, OK 74018-2104. (918) 342-
1080.

Geraniums

This unusual windowsill planter, which my father designed, has a multitude of uses. Not only is it classy when holding your favorite potted plant, but it quickly converts to a bread basket for your outdoor barbeque, or will easily hold six dozen of your favorite cookies.

BACKGROUND PREPARATION

Seal with Designs From the Heart wood sealer, and sand. Paint the ends of the box with Accent Country Colors Deep Forest Green. Paint a trim panel on each side using the same color. Stain the remainder of the box with BU thinned with odorless brush cleaner. Spray with Krylon Matte Finish, no. 1311.

PALETTE
Winsor & Newton Alkyd or Oil Colors:

Burnt Umber (BU), Cadmium Lemon (CL), Ivory Black (BLK), Cadmium Red Light (CRL), Yellow Ochre (YO), Titanium White (TW), Cadmium Yellow Medium (CYM), Cadmium Red Medium (CRM), Dioxazine Purple (DP), Prussian Blue (PB), Raw Sienna (RS)—oil only

Rembrandt Oil Colors:
Naples Yellow Deep Extra (NYD), Naples Yellow Light Extra (NYL)

Grumbacher Oil Color:
Geranium Lake (GL)

MIDVALUE GERANIUM
Dark Area . . . . .GL + BLK
Light Area . . . . .CRL + YO
Shade . . . . .Dark area mix + BLK
Highlight . . . . . .NYD
　　　　　　　　　NYL
　　　　　　　　　TW
Tint . . . . .BLK + TW
　　　　　　　　　CYM

LIGHTEST GERANIUM
Dark Area . . . . .CRL + RS
Light Area . . . . .Dark area mix + NYD
Shade . . . . .GL + RS
Highlight . . . . . .NYD
　　　　　　　　　NYL

DARKEST GERANIUM
Dark Area . . . . .GL + BLK
Light Area . . . . .CRM
Shade . . . . .Dark area mix + DP
Highlight . . . . . .CRL
Tint . . . . .BLK + TW

FLOWER CENTERS
Green mixtures
CYM

LEAVES
Dark Area . . . . .BLK + CL + PB
Light Area . . . . .CL + BLK + TW
Shade . . . . .Dark area mix + BLK
Highlight . . . . . .CL + TW
　　　　　　　　　TW
Accent . . . . .GL + RS
　　　　　　　　　GL + RS + DP

In painting this design, it is important to keep the midvalue red flower in the foreground in order to create a center of interest. To achieve this, add a few CYM tints to the flower petals in the foreground. Warm colors bring an area of the design forward. Use the BLK + TW tint on the receding petals in this flower. Notice also that a few of the flowerlets are brighter and have stronger highlights. Each of these details will help produce value, shape and dimension.

Also remember that where the petals overlap and a triangular area is formed, you want the shading to be very dark. If necessary, apply this color several times to achieve maximum depth.

The red accents were placed on the leaves after they were dry. Glaze them with a very small amount of Winsor & Newton Blending & Glazing Medium and apply the color sparingly. The large front leaf was accented with GL + RS, a rich, warm red, which will bring this leaf into the foreground. The other leaves should appear cooler; therefore, DP was added to the accent.

Heart basket available from GCP Enterprises, P.O. Box 2104, Claremore, OK 74018-2104. (918) 342-1080.

Geraniums

Coral Elegance

Coral Elegance

BACKGROUND PREPARATION

Seal all surface areas with Designs From the Heart wood sealer, and sand when dry. Paint the sides of the vanity, drawer front, edges of the panels and the mirror supports with Delta Avocado. Spray-seal these areas with Krylon Matte Finish, no. 1311, and then antique them with a wash of BU plus a small touch of odorless brush cleaner. Paint the front panel frames with Delta Light Red Oxide and then gold leaf these areas. Paint inside the panels and the mirror frame with an off-white acrylic paint. Trace the pattern for the inside panel, turn the tracing to the reverse side and retrace with a no. 2 pencil. Apply the penciled side to the surface and trace over the pattern lines again. Using a technical pen, ink the design. Clean off any pencil marks with clean, odorless brush cleaner. Spray-seal these panels with Krylon Matte Finish, no. 1311. Soft tint work was done around the flowers.

PALETTE

Winsor & Newton Alkyd or Oil Colors:

Burnt Umber (BU), Light Red Oxide (LRO), Cadmium Red Light (CRL), Yellow Ochre (YO), Titanium White (TW), French Ultramarine (FU), Dioxazine Purple (DP), Cadmium Lemon (CL), Sap Green (SG), Olive Green (OG), Winsor Orange (WO), Raw Sienna (RS)—oil only

Rembrandt Oil Colors:

Naples Yellow Deep Extra (NYD), Naples Yellow Light Extra (NYL), Greenish Umber (GU), Transparent Oxide Red (TOR)

Grumbacher Oil Color:

Geranium Lake (GL)

LARGE BOTTOM RIGHT BLOSSOM

Dark Area . . . . .LRO
Midvalue . . . . . .WO
     CRL + YO
Light Area . . . .NYD
     NYL
Shade . . . . .GL + TOR
Highlight . . . . . .TW
Tint . . . . .BLK + TW

UPPER RIGHT BLOSSOM

Base . . . . .NYL + LRO
Shade . . . . . . .LRO + CRL
     TOR + GL
Highlight . . . . . .TW
Tint . . . . .NYD
     BLK + TW

LOWER LEFT POPPY

Base . . . . .LRO
Highlight . . . . . .CRL
     WO
     NYD
     NYL
     TW
Shade . . . . .GL + TOR
     GL + BLK

UPPER LEFT POPPY

Use same colors as for darker poppy, but build highlights much lighter.

CENTER

Base . . . . .FU + DP +
     small amount
     BLK
Highlight . . . . . .TW

DOTS

Dark Area . . . . .BLK + DP +
     FU
Light Area . . . . .Dark area mix +
     TW

LEAF #1

Base . . . . .BLK + CL +
     TW
Shade . . . . .BLK + CL
Highlight . . . . . .TW

LEAF #2

Dark Area . . . . .BLK + CL
Light Area . . . . .Dark area mix +
     CL + TW
Shade . . . . .FU + DP +
     BLK
Highlight . . . . . .TW + small
     amount CL

BACKGROUND BEHIND PAINTED POPPIES

Use your darker green leaf colors behind the flowers and leaves. Add more CL and TW as you come to the lighter areas on the inside of the panels. The lightest color is BLK + TW.

FILLER FLOWERS

DP + FU + BLK
LRO
LRO + NYD
LRO + NYL
NYD
DP + FU + BLK + TW
NYL

INKED POPPIES

Use same colors as for painted poppies. Use very small amounts of paint, with Winsor & Newton Blending & Glazing Medium if necessary, to give a soft, tinted look.

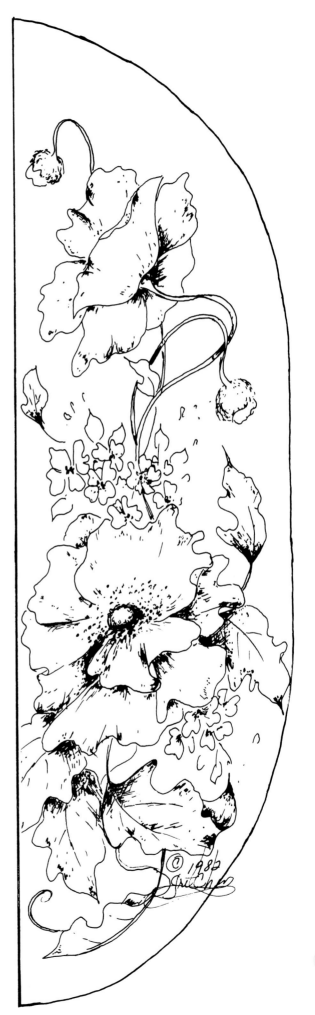

Coral Elegance

Center
Same colors as for painted poppies.

Leaves
Tint with various mixtures of SG, GU and OG, adding BLK or RS for different values. I used a cotton swab to clean out the highlights.

Background
Tint darker green behind the leaves and let fade out. Flyspeck with darker greens and RS.

Vanity chest available from GCP Enterprises, P.O. Box 2104, Claremore, OK 74018-2104. (918)-342-1080.

Pattern for inside of doors. Reverse for right side.

Index